CAMBRIDGE LIBRARY COLLECTION

Books of enduring scholarly value

Egyptology

The large-scale scientific investigation of Egyptian antiquities by Western scholars began as an unintended consequence of Napoleon's invasion of Egypt during which, in 1799, the Rosetta Stone was discovered. The military expedition was accompanied by French scholars, whose reports prompted a wave of enthusiasm that swept across Europe and North America resulting in the Egyptian Revival style in art and architecture. Increasing numbers of tourists visited Egypt, eager to see the marvels being revealed by archaeological excavation. Writers and booksellers responded to this growing interest with publications ranging from technical site reports to tourist guidebooks and from children's histories to theories identifying the pyramids as repositories of esoteric knowledge. This series reissues a wide selection of such books. They reveal the gradual change from the 'tomb-robbing' approach of early excavators to the highly organised and systematic approach of Flinders Petrie, the 'father of Egyptology', and include early accounts of the decipherment of the hieroglyphic script.

The History of Egypt under the Ptolemies

This 1838 work by Samuel Sharpe (1799–1881) is the second of two volumes on the history of ancient Egypt: the first, dealing with the earlier period, is also reissued in this series. From a banking family, Sharpe was fascinated by Young's and Champollion's work in deciphering the hieroglyphs. He taught himself Coptic, and compiled his own hieroglyphic vocabulary lists. His facility for decipherment was assisted by a natural gift for solving cryptograms, but his inferences sometimes led him into error. This book, in which Sharpe follows his earlier technique of using inscriptions as well as historical works as sources, begins with a survey of the history of Egypt up to the time of Alexander the Great: the interested reader is referred to Sharpe's earlier volume for more details. He then surveys the Ptolemaic era by reigns, ending with the battle of Actium and the conquest of Egypt by Augustus.

Cambridge University Press has long been a pioneer in the reissuing of out-of-print titles from its own backlist, producing digital reprints of books that are still sought after by scholars and students but could not be reprinted economically using traditional technology. The Cambridge Library Collection extends this activity to a wider range of books which are still of importance to researchers and professionals, either for the source material they contain, or as landmarks in the history of their academic discipline.

Drawing from the world-renowned collections in the Cambridge University Library and other partner libraries, and guided by the advice of experts in each subject area, Cambridge University Press is using state-of-the-art scanning machines in its own Printing House to capture the content of each book selected for inclusion. The files are processed to give a consistently clear, crisp image, and the books finished to the high quality standard for which the Press is recognised around the world. The latest print-on-demand technology ensures that the books will remain available indefinitely, and that orders for single or multiple copies can quickly be supplied.

The Cambridge Library Collection brings back to life books of enduring scholarly value (including out-of-copyright works originally issued by other publishers) across a wide range of disciplines in the humanities and social sciences and in science and technology.

The History of Egypt under the Ptolemies

Samuel Sharpe

CAMBRIDGE
UNIVERSITY PRESS

University Printing House, Cambridge, CB2 8BS, United Kingdom

Cambridge University Press is part of the University of Cambridge.

It furthers the University's mission by disseminating knowledge in the pursuit of
education, learning and research at the highest international levels of excellence.

www.cambridge.org
Information on this title: www.cambridge.org/9781108082976

© in this compilation Cambridge University Press 2015

This edition first published 1838
This digitally printed version 2015

ISBN 978-1-108-08297-6 Paperback

THE

HISTORY

OF

EGYPT

UNDER

THE PTOLEMIES.

BY

SAMUEL SHARPE.

LONDON:

EDWARD MOXON, DOVER STREET.

1838.

TO THE READER.

THE Author has given neither the arguments nor the whole of the authorities on which the sketch of the earlier history in the Introduction rests, as it would have had too much of the dryness of an antiquarian enquiry, and as he has already published them in his Early History of Egypt. In the rest of the book he has in every case pointed out in the margin the sources from which he has drawn his information.

Canonbury, 12th November, 1838.

Works published by the same Author.

The EARLY HISTORY of EGYPT, from the Old Testament, Herodotus, Manetho, and the Hieroglyphical Inscriptions.

EGYPTIAN INSCRIPTIONS, from the British Museum and other sources. Sixty Plates in folio.

Rudiments of a VOCABULARY of EGYPTIAN HIEROGLYPHICS.

ERRATA.

Page 103, line 23, *for* Syria *read* Macedonia.
Page 104, line 4, *for* Syrians *read* Macedonians.

CONTENTS.

THE HISTORY OF EGYPT

UNDER THE PTOLEMIES.

INTRODUCTION.

WHEN letters first rose in Greece and Rome, the writers found a rich harvest of fable and tradition, out of which they wove those beautiful tales that we now read as the beginning of Greek and Roman history. The Egyptians were not favoured with historians who could thus fix and hand down to us their traditions; but, on the other hand, they had from far earlier times carved the names and deeds of their kings on the granite temples, and thus, instead of a rich poetic fable, they have left us a bald reality.

In each case, the history of the country begins with scattered and dark hints, which some minds seize upon as treasures and others overlook as worthless, but which the historian can neither safely lean upon nor yet wholly fling from him; and this is the case with the history of Egypt before the time when Abraham drove his herds into that country in search of food, which the drought had made scarce in Canaan.

Egypt was then broken up into several little kingdoms. Upper Egypt, the most powerful of these, had been ruled over by a race of kings who reigned in This, a city near the spot, or perhaps on the spot, where Abydos afterwards stood; and who had held Thebes, and

Manetho.

some of them Memphis, as part of their kingdom. We are told the names of seventeen who reigned in This; after which that city fell, and Thebes rose to be capital of Upper Egypt; and it was perhaps in the reign of the second or third Theban king that Abraham entered the Delta.

The city of Elephantine, on an island in the Nile, just below the cataract at the southern boundary of Egypt, was also the capital of a little kingdom; and we know the names, and nothing but the names, of nine kings who had reigned there. Elephantine no doubt fell when Thebes rose over the city of This.

Memphis was the capital of the rich corn-fields of Lower Egypt, or the land of Mizraim as it is called in the Old Testament; and perhaps the tenth of those Memphite kings whose names are known to us was reigning in the time of Abraham.

We likewise have the name of one king who reigned at Heracleopolis; and, as that city is close to Memphis, it is most likely that he ruled over Memphis, and made Heracleopolis the capital of Lower Egypt during his reign.

The people of both Upper and Lower Egypt seem to have been Copts, children of Cham or Ham, and from him they called their country Chemi; and they spoke a language which, after it has undergone the changes of so many ages, we even now know as Coptic. Their religion was the same as what Herodotus and Diodorus afterwards found there: many cities had already their sacred animals; the bull Apis in Memphis, the bull Mnevis in Heliopolis, and the goat Mando in Mendes, were fed and waited upon at the cost of those cities, and worshipped as images of Chem, or Amun-Ra, the Sun.

Their buildings were much the same as those which afterwards rose in such massive grandeur. Venephres, king of This, had already built pyramids at a city named Cochome ; the older part of the great temple of Thebes, now called the temple of Karnak, was already begun ; and Abraham most likely saw the obelisk of Osirtesen I., which even yet stands at Heliopolis.

Wilkinson's
Thebes.

The carved writing, by means of figures of men and animals, which was afterwards, when easier ways of writing came into use, called sacred carving, or hieroglyphics, was even then not new. The inscriptions of the Osirtesens do not show us hieroglyphics in their earliest form ; in them we see many words spelt alphabetically mixt up with the symbols or pictures of objects and actions. There had been, most likely, many ages before their time during which the hieroglyphics were wholly symbolic, before alphabetic spelling had been thought of.

Egypt.Inscrip.
plate 6.

The journey of Abraham into Egypt was not that of a single family ; there was at the same time a great migration going on, of Phenicians, moving out of their own country into Lower Egypt, and along the African coast of the Mediterranean. We shall hereafter see that the Greek settlers at Cyrene had to drive them back from the coast, and tradition says that Phenician Dido was kindly received by them at Carthage. They were peaceably driven out of Canaan by other troops of herdsmen who were moving westward from Chaldæa and Mesopotamia, and who made the pasture-land too crowded for their loose and scattered way of life.

Manetho.

Pausanias,
lib. i. 7.

Gen. xi.

Abraham found Lower Egypt a well-tilled corn country; the king, or Pharaoh, was surrounded by princes and servants, and was by no means looked upon by Abraham as his equal, as the little kings of Canaan had been.

Gen. xii.

Abraham did not remain long in Lower Egypt ; from the head of the Red Sea he went southward, and returned home by Mount Sinai and Petra ; but the Phenicians settled in crowds in the Delta, and may have been a cause of great wealth to the country, as about that time Suphis, and his brother and successor Sensuphis, who were Coptic kings of Memphis, were strong enough to conquer Thebes, and rich enough to build the two largest of the pyramids near Memphis.

But the Phenicians soon got too strong for the country which had given them a home; they chose a king of their own, named Salatis, who at first ruled over his countrymen without rebelling against the Egyptians; but he afterwards seized Memphis, and from thence sent forth his armed bands, each year, at harvest time, to gather in a duty upon corn, and the pay for his troops. He had an army of two hundred and forty thousand men; and he strongly fortified the city of Avaris, perhaps that afterwards called Pelusium, as a frontier town against the Assyrians. In the third or fourth reign of these Phenician shepherds, or herdsmen, or Hycsos as they were called by the Egyptians, they even conquered Thebes, and reigned over all Egypt.

It was in the reign of Apophis, one of these Phenicians, when the two countries of Canaan and Lower Egypt were filled by the same people, that, among other slaves brought into Egypt by the cara- vans from the east, was a young Jew named Joseph, who chanced to be sold into the service of the captain of the guard. Little could his master have foreseen the coming greatness of his slave, or how much his name would be known in after ages.

Joseph soon rose to the head of his master's household, and afterwards to be the king's chief minister. He foresaw a scarcity of corn, and bought up the harvest in years of plenty; and with these stores, in the years of scarcity, he bought from the starving Egyptians the freeholds of their estates, which he afterwards let them hold as tenants of the crown, at a rent of one-fifth of the crop. The priests, however, were allowed to keep their freeholds, as being a privileged order in the state.

Thus this Asiatic minister made the king the landlord of the country, and the land was held by what is now known in Asia as the Ryot tenure. But in Asia the farmers are tenants at a changeable rack-rent of about one-half of the crop; whereas the Egyptians paid a fixt and low rent of one-fifth. The Egyptian landholder was therefore rich enough to have peasants or slaves under him, while the Indian Ryot is himself the peasant-tenant of the crown. This rent was in the place of all direct taxes, and, except the duties upon manufactures, and upon the exports and imports, no other tax was laid upon Egypt till it was conquered by the Persians.

Jones on Rent.

Asseth, one of these Phenician kings, is said to have brought, no doubt from Babylon the birth-place of astronomy, a better knowledge of the length of the year than was then found in Egypt. The Egyptian year had been divided into twelve months of thirty days each, and Asseth, without altering the months, added to the end of the year five days, which were called by the Greeks the *epagomenæ*. But this change in the calendar seems not to have been generally received till a hundred years later, when it was ordered by one of the Coptic kings of Thebes.

Manetho.

Soon after the death of Apophis, the kings of Thebes and Memphis made common cause against the Phenicians, and, driving them out of the rest of the country, blocked up their forces in the strong city of Avaris. Here they were besieged by Amosis king of Thebes, and then driven through the desert into Syria, where they built the city of Jerusalem, while the unarmed part of the nation remained as slaves in Lower Egypt.

From this time we find Upper Egypt rising in wealth and power; and though we are still told the names of the kings of Memphis, they seem to have been under the sceptre of their more powerful

Wilkinson's Thebes.

Theban neighbours. The inscriptions of the reigns of Amun-mai Thor II. and Osirtesen II., at Cosseir, the port on the Red Sea which is nearest to Thebes, prove that the trade to Arabia and across Arabia had begun even before the Phenicians had been driven out of Egypt.

Manetho.

Chebros, the son of Amosis, reigned after him; and the Jews, who had been well treated in the Delta in grateful recollection of

Exodus, i. 8.

the services of Joseph, now began to be harshly used by the Theban kings; task-masters were set over them, and they were cruelly

i. 11.

over-worked at the fortifications of Memphis and Heliopolis, and at the other buildings of Lower Egypt.

Amunothph I., the son-in-law of Chebros, reigned next. He is the first of the kings whose tombs are now found in the Valley of Tombs near Thebes. These royal burial-places are tunnelled into the side of the hills, and are wide and lofty rooms, whose ceilings are upheld by columns, and whose walls are covered with paintings

Wilkinson's Thebes.

and sculptures. In the tomb of Amunothph I. are well-formed statues, and sculptures in high relief; on one of the walls is painted a funeral procession by water, with a mummy lying in one of the boats, which shows how very early were the customs both of making mummies and of ferrying the dead over the river, which Diodorus saw in use thirteen hundred years later, and from which the Greeks borrowed the boat of Charon.

Mesphra-Thothmosis I. made some additions to the great temple at Thebes, which had been begun by Osirtesen I.; he also built at Tombos in Ethiopia, whence we learn that part of that country had already been brought under the sceptre of Egypt.

Amun-Nitocris, or Neit-thor (for the guttural is written either with a TH or a C), the last Memphite sovereign, then reigned over Thebes. Eratosthenes says that she reigned for her husband. She was handsome among women and brave among men, and one of the more powerful sovereigns of Egypt; she was a great builder, and set up two obelisks and two small temples at Thebes, and built the smallest of the three large pyramids near Memphis. Henceforth all Egypt was under one sceptre.

Mesphra-Thothmosis II. was most likely the husband of Nitocris; he outlived her, and in many cases had her name cut out of the monuments, and his own carved in the place of it. He added to the buildings at Thebes, and built at Samneh in Ethiopia.

Thothmosis III. also added to the buildings at Thebes, and built at Memphis, at Heliopolis, at Samneh, and at Talmis in Ethiopia. In his tomb at Thebes, which, like those of the other kings, is a set of spacious rooms tunnelled into the hill, is a painting of men of the several conquered nations bringing gifts to the king. There are Egyptians; there are negroes bearing ivory, apes, and leopard-skins; there are Ethiopians with rings, hides, apes, leopards, ivory, ostrich-eggs and feathers, a camelopard, hounds with handsome collars, and long-horned oxen; and there are men of a white nation, with short beards and white dresses, bringing gloves, vases, a bear, an elephant, and a chariot with horses. At Thebes there is a brick arch with this king's name upon it; and, though there are vaulted rooms of an earlier time, this is perhaps the earliest arch known.

There are two chains of reasoning by which we may hope to fix the date of this reign: first, Herodotus says that Mœris, a king who governed Memphis, lived nine hundred years before his time; secondly, Theon says that Menophres was king when the calendar was reformed, and when the dog-star rose heliacally on the first day of

Wilkinson's Thebes.

the month of Thoth, or B.C. 1321. On which we remark—first, that Mœris and Menophres were most likely a Thothmosis, as they are nearer to Mesphres than to any other name; second, that the figure of Thothmosis III. is often drawn with a palm-branch, the hieroglyphic for 'year,' in each hand, which may be meant to point out that he made some change in the length of the civil year; third, that Plutarch says that the god Thoth, who may in this case have been meant for Thothmosis, taught the Egyptians the true length of the year. These reasons are perhaps not very strong; but in a part of the history where we find so few traces of chronology, we follow any thing which seems as if it would guide us.

Wilkinson's Thebes.

Amunothph II. has left his name upon temples at Apollinopolis Parva, at Eilethyas, and at Elephantine, of all of which he was most likely the builder. The sculptures in his tomb are in the best style of Egyptian art, for borders, for vases, and for the human figure.

Manetho.

This seems to have been the king who drove the Israelites out of Egypt. He was warned by the priests, says the Egyptian historian, to cleanse the country of the lepers who were working in the quarries on the east side of the Nile. They had then risen in arms under the guidance of a priest of Heliopolis, named Osarsiph [or Joseph], who afterwards changed his name to Moses. He made laws for his countrymen, and bound them by an oath not to worship the gods and sacred animals of Egypt.

Exodus, xii.37.

The Jews marched out of the Delta, in number six hundred thousand men, beside women and children. After leaving the head of the Red Sea, they turned southward, along the coast, to Mount Sinai, and then northward, by Petra, towards Canaan; and with them went out a crowd of Arabs, who were part of the Phenician herdsmen of the Delta, and who are called Mixed People by the Jewish writers.

Thothmosis IV. built the small temple between the fore-legs of Hieroglyphics plate 80. the great Sphinx near Memphis; but it may be doubted whether the rock was carved into the form of this huge monster in his reign, or at an earlier time. He built at El Berkel, the capital of Ethio- Wilkinson's Thebes. pia; and in the sculptures on the walls of a temple at Silsilis he is being carried in a palanquin, surrounded by his fan-bearers, and receiving the gifts of the conquered nations.

Amunothph III. seems to have built more in Ethiopia than any other Egyptian king; he also began the temple of Luxor; but he is most known by his colossal statue at Thebes, called the statue of Memnon, which is sixty feet high though sitting, and which Strabo, Pausanias, and so many other Greek and Roman travellers, heard utter its far-famed musical sounds at sunrise.

Of Amunmai Anamek we know little beyond his statue in the British Museum; and of Rameses I. nothing but his tomb at Thebes.

Amunmai Amunaan, or Osirei I., began the palaces at Abydos and at Old Quorneh, and made great additions to the temple of Karnak. The whole of his sculptures and buildings are remarkably beautiful, and in the best style of art. His tomb is at Thebes; and the sarcophagus which it once held is now in Sir John Soane's museum.

This king seems to have been successful in his wars, and among the paintings on the walls of his tomb is a procession of the several conquered nations bringing their gifts.

Rameses II., or the Great, was the king under whom Egypt reached its greatest height in arms, in arts, and in wealth. His palace at Thebes yielded to no building in the world for beauty and costliness. Its spacious rooms, in the middle open to the sky, but with roofs resting upon columns round the sides, were standing in Diod. Sic. lib. i. all their glory when Hecatæus travelled in Upper Egypt, and its

ruins are even now looked at with wonder by our travellers : it was
called the Memnonium, from the king's first name, Amun-mai, or
Mi-amun, which the Greeks changed into Memnon. He added to
the temple of Luxor, and set up two obelisks in front of it, one of
which is now at Paris. The temple of Osiris, and the palace called
the Memnonium at Abydos, which were begun by his father, were
for the most part built in this reign. His statues and obelisks are
found in all parts of Egypt, and lead us to call this the Augustan,
or when speaking of Egypt we ought perhaps to say the Philadelphian, age of Coptic art : it had reached its greatest beauty, and
was not yet overloaded with ornament.

The sculptures on the walls of the Memnonium at Thebes show
the king's victories over people of the Tartar, Arab, Ethiopian, and
Negro races ; and the hieroglyphics, which were read to Germanicus by one of the priests, recounted his conquests of the Libyans,
Ethiopians, Medes, Persians, Bactrians, Scythians, Syrians, Arme-
nians, Cappadocians, Bithynians, and Lycians, together with the
weight of gold and silver, and the other gifts, which these nations
sent to Thebes as their yearly tribute.

Tacitus,
Annal. lib. ii.

The population of the country may be counted at five millions
and a half, as there were seven hundred thousand men able to carry
arms ; and the gold and silver mines alone were said to bring in
each year the unheard-of sum of three million two hundred thousand minæ, or seven millions sterling.

Diod. Sic.
lib. i. 49.

After the reigns of three other kings, about whom we know but
little, came Rameses III., whose palace at Medinet Abu, and other
buildings and historical sculptures, prove that his reign fell very
little short of that of Rameses II. in wealth and conquests.

He was followed by eight or ten other kings of the family, and
most of them of the name, of Rameses ; but, during their reigns,

Upper Egypt was falling and Lower Egypt rising in trade and power. Few of these kings held Lower Egypt; some were even vassals of the kings who then rose in Tanis and Bubastus; and when the Grecian chiefs were fighting against Troy, before Homer had called Egyptian Thebes the richest and greatest city in the world, its glory had already passed—its sun had set even before the day-break of Greek history; and before the Jebusites had been conquered by David, and Jerusalem made the capital of Judæa, Thebes had ceased to give laws to Egypt.

We are unable to show how the line of Theban kings joins that of Lower Egypt; but the first king of Lower Egypt who sat upon the throne of Rameses was Shishank of Bubastus, who has left the B.C. 970. history of his conquests in Asia and Ethiopia carved upon the great temple of Karnak, by the side of those of Rameses II.; and on the figure of one of the conquered kings is written 'The king of Judah,' in boast of his well-known conquest of Rehoboam. 2 Chron. xii.

Solomon had married the daughter of an Egyptian king, most 1 Kings, ix. likely of Shishank, who, having taken the city of Gaza, gave it to his son-in-law as his daughter's dower.

The trade of Thebes seems to have been at all times large. When navigation by sea was dangerous and little known, and not so cheap as caravans through the desert, there was no carrying trade in the world that could vie for ease and speed with that on the Nile, which brought the wealth of India and Arabia from the ports on the Red Sea to the coasting vessels of the Mediterranean. But when Memphis was at war with Thebes the trade of the Nile was stopt, and the caravans of Arabia then sought Jerusalem and Tyre, through the city of Petra; and Solomon and Hiram fitted out their ships on the Red Sea.

Thebes never regained the power which it then lost. Its crowded population had been fed by the rich corn-fields of the Delta, its priests and nobles had been enriched by the tributes of its foreign provinces, and by the trade which floated upon the Nile: it lost every thing when it lost Lower Egypt, and it soon found itself unable to hold Ethiopia.

Herodotus,
lib. ii.

Shishank, also, if he was the same king as the Sesostris of Herodotus, overran Scythia and Thrace, and on his return home left a body of troops behind him, who founded the city of Colchis. He also tried to gain part of the trade of the Red Sea for Lower Egypt, by making a ship-canal between Suez and the nearest branch of the

Aristoteles,
de Rep. vii. 10.

Nile, but he was unable to finish the work. He set apart the soldiers as a privileged order in the state, as the priests had been since the time of Joseph.

Manetho.

Osorkon I. followed his father Shishank, and also held Thebes; and after him some of the kings of the name of Rameses may have

B.C. 900.

regained the throne of their fathers. But in a few years Takelothe, a king of Bubastus, is again reigning at Thebes.

Manetho.

Osorkon II., Shishank II., and other kings of Tanis, then governed Egypt; and after them Bocchoris of Sais, one of the great Egyptian lawgivers; and it was no doubt from the weakness brought upon the country by these civil wars and changes that Egypt then fell an easy prey to the Ethiopians.

Wilkinson's
Thebes.

The three kings of Ethiopia who held Egypt have left their names carved in hieroglyphics on the temples of Thebes; and were most likely of the same race, spoke the same tongue, and worshipped

Manetho.

the same gods, as the other kings of Egypt. Sabacon, the first of them, conquered Thebes, Memphis, and Sais,—while the last of the kings of Tanis still held out in his own city; but Sevechus, or

So, was master of the whole of Egypt, and was courted by Hoshea 2 Kings, xvii.
B.C. 729. king of Israel, when he was in danger from his warlike neighbour the king of Assyria, because the Jews had left off paying the yearly tribute. The Assyrians, however, overran Judæa, and the Egyptian alliance was broken; and though Tirhakah, the third Ethiopian king of Egypt, threatened to march against Palestine, he does not seem to have done so.

On the fall of the Ethiopians, the kings of Sais gained the mas- Manetho. tery of Egypt; and under them the population, the trade, and the power of the country were very great; but, as their thoughts and wealth were not turned towards building or the arts, we have now but few traces of their greatness.

Nechepsus, the first of the Saïtic kings, has left a name known Ausonius,
Ep. 409, 20. for his priestly learning; and his astronomical writings are quoted by Pliny. He was followed by Necho I., Psammetichus I., and Pliny, lib. ii. Necho II. The last stretched his arms from Ethiopia to the Euphrates, and slew Josiah king of Judah at Megiddo; and, when the 2 Kings, xxiii.
B.C. 608. Jews made Jehoahaz king, he took him prisoner, and made Eliakim, the elder brother, king in his place; and he made Judæa pay a yearly tribute to Egypt of one hundred talents of silver and one talent of gold, or about twenty thousand pounds sterling. But, five years Jeremiah,xlvi. afterwards, Necho was beaten in pitched battle by Nebuchadnezzar, and lost all that had belonged to Egypt between the Euphrates and the Nile.

Necho sent some Phenicians on a voyage of discovery, to circum- Herodotus,
lib. ii. navigate Africa; they set sail down the Red Sea, and after a coasting voyage of two years, they again reached Egypt, through the Straits of Gibraltar. The account which they gave of what they saw, and which made Herodotus distrust the story, is the best proof that the voyage was really performed : they said that as they sailed towards the west the sun was on their right hand. This could only have been true on the south side of the equator.

We do not know by what soldiers Shishank and the other kings of Lower Egypt overthrew the hardy troops of Rameses ; but, as the Greeks had from the earliest time settled in the ports of the Delta, and had already proved to the world and to themselves their skill in arms, they most likely formed part of the armies. At any rate the throne of these Saïtic kings was upheld by Greek swords ; and a Greek inscription at Aboo Simbal, in Ethiopia, proves that the Ionian and Carian mercenaries guarded the southern border of the kingdom of Psammetichus II., who then came to the throne.

Herodotus, lib. ii., and Jeremiah, xxxvii.

Apries, or Hophra, succeeded ; and to him Zedekiah sent for help when Nebuchadnezzar laid siege to Jerusalem. Apries led his army against Sidon, and sent his fleet against Tyre, and the Chaldees raised the siege. But in the twenty-fifth year of his reign, when his army was beaten in an attack upon Cyrene, the Egyptians set up Amasis as king ; and though the Carians and Ionians stood faithful to Apries, he was overthrown and put to death by Amasis and the native troops.

Herodotus, lib. ii.

Amasis built a temple to Isis at Memphis, and added to the temple of Neith at Sais. He cultivated the friendship of the Greeks, and gave the city of Naucratis, on the Canobic mouth of the Nile, to those who chose to settle there, and gave them great commercial privileges. At Naucratis the several cities of Greece built temples to Jupiter, Juno, and Apollo ; and one, called the Grecian temple, was built at the joint cost of many cities.

Amasis conquered the island of Cyprus, which continued for so many years afterwards a part of Egypt. He is said to have married a daughter of Battus king of Cyrene ; but we have in the British

Museum the sarcophagus of one of his wives, a daughter of Psam- Egypt.Inscrip. plate 58.
metichus.

Under the favour now shown to the Greeks, Solon the Athenian Plutarch. in Solone.
lawgiver visited Egypt, and, while carrying on his trade of an oil- Herodotus, lib. i. 30.
merchant, studied the manners and customs of the country; and
from the Egyptians he copied the law, that every man should be
called upon by the magistrate to give an account of how he earned
his livelihood. Pythagoras also studied in Egypt, and may have
there learnt his doctrine of the transmigration of the soul after
death into a new body. He may also have gained in Egypt his
mathematical knowledge, by which he afterwards found out his
famous proposition of the square of the hypothenuse being equal
to the squares of the other sides in a right-angled triangle.

Psammenitus succeeded his father Amasis, but his reign was short Herodotus, lib. ii. B.C. 525.
and unfortunate. Cambyses king of Persia marched against Egypt
at the head of a large army; on his approach, Phanes, with a body
of Greek mercenaries, went over to him, and he overthrew the
Egyptian army, with the rest of the Greeks, near Pelusium; he
then took Memphis and Sais, and put Psammenitus to death within
six months of his coming to the throne.

Thus ended the dynasties of Lower Egypt, which had lasted,
though not without a break, for four hundred years, beginning with
the reign of Shishank. They had long stood by the help of Greek
mercenaries, and they fell when the Greeks under Phanes went lib. iii.
over to the Persians.

Cambyses governed the Egyptians with the harshness and cruelty
of a conqueror; he ill-treated the nobles, scourged the priests,
laughed at their religion, killed the sacred bull Apis with his own
hand, and carried away with him all the gold and silver that he

could find in the temples. He made Egypt a Persian province, and put it under a satrap, whose duty it was to squeeze the country of its wealth for the benefit of Persia.

Herodotus,
lib. vii. 1—7.
B.C. 517.
Darius Hystaspes was so far taken up with his wars with Greece that, in the fourth year of his reign, the Egyptians were able to throw off the Persian yoke. They do not however seem to have set up a king of their own, but for thirty-four years continued in name under the sceptre of Persia. A temple built in the great oasis during this reign bears the name of Darius, and the ship-canal, from the Red Sea to the Nile near Pelusium, was at last finished; but we know not whether the well-being of Egypt, at this time, arose from its successful rebellion or from the mild treatment of its foreign king.

lib. vii. 7.
B.C. 485.
Xerxes, in the second year of his reign, again made Egypt bend under the Persian yoke, and sent his brother Achæmenes as satrap of the province.

Thucydides,
lib. i.
B.C. 461.
In the beginning of the reign of Artaxerxes, Inarus king of Libya was successful in raising Egypt against Persia, and called in the Athenians to his help. They sailed from Cyprus in two hundred ships, and blockaded the Persians in a part of Memphis called the White Wall.

Artaxerxes then sent to Sparta, to try to get the Athenians called home by an attack of the Lacedemonians on Athens. The Lacedemonians were unsuccessful; but Megabazus, the Persian general, reconquered Egypt, and put Inarus to death. Some of the Egyptians however still held out, in the marshes of the Delta, against the Persian forces, and neither Artaxerxes, nor Darius Nothus after him, were able to conquer them.

It was in the reign of Artaxerxes that Herodotus, the father of history, visited Egypt, and was as much struck by the high state to which the arts and sciences had been there carried as by the wonders of the Sphinx and pyramids; and he carried back to Greece the doctrine, before unheard of, of the immortality of the soul and a life after death. His description of the country, the people, and their religion is in the highest degree curious; but, as he seems to have learnt nothing from the priests of Memphis about the early kings, except those who were natives of the Delta, his history is only valuable for the kings of the Saïtic dynasty.

About the same time, though most likely a little earlier, Hellanicus visited Egypt. He wrote a description of the country, which was to be met with in the libraries of Alexandria for above six hundred years, but is since lost. *A. Gellius, lib. xv. 23. Athenæus, lib. xi. 6.*

In the reign of Darius Nothus, the Persians were again driven out of Egypt; and Amyrtæus of Sais, who had for some little time been reigning in the marshes, made himself king, and the country was once more free. He reigned quietly for six years; he added to the buildings in Thebes, and in the great oasis; he set up an obelisk at Memphis; and the beautiful sarcophagus in which he was buried is now lying in the British Museum. *Manetho. B.C. 414.*

Pausiris, his son, succeeded him, but rather as a satrap of Persia than as a king; and we next find five kings of Mendes following one another on the throne of Egypt: Nepherites, Achoris, Psammuthes, Muthes, and Nepherites. They were in league with Cyprus, and were sometimes helped by the Athenians against the Persians. *Herodotus, lib. iii. 15. B.C. 408. Manetho. Diod. Sic. lib. xv.*

Nectanebo I., of Sebennytus, then reigned over Egypt, and Artaxerxes Mnemon sent against him an army of two hundred thousand men under his general Pharnabazus, with twenty thousand Greeks under Iphicrates of Athens. But the overflow of the Nile, and the jealousy between the generals, defeated this expedition. *B.C. 377.*

Diogenes
Laertius;
and Strabo,
lib. xvii.
In this reign Eudoxus the astronomer, Chrysippus the physician, and Plato, the still more famous philosopher, came to Egypt with friendly letters from Agesilaus king of Sparta, to Nectanebo and the priests. Of the schools of Egypt at this time we unfortunately know nothing; but we can have no greater proof of the esteem in which they were held, than that these three men, each at the head of his own branch of science, should have come to Egypt to finish Diog. Laert.
viii. 90. their studies. Here Eudoxus may have learnt from Ichonuphys of Heliopolis, under whom he studied, the true length of the year and of the month, upon which he formed his octaëterid, a period of eight years or ninety-nine months; Chrysippus may have learnt anatomy, which the prejudices of the Greeks forbad him to study at home; and Plato may have learnt the doctrine of the immortality of the soul.

We find the name of Nectanebo on the buildings of Thebes and of the island of Philæ, which shows that the arts were not wholly dead in this reign.

Diod. Sic.
lib. xv. 92.
Teos, or Tachus, then succeeded; but he had to defend his throne against the power of the Persians, who still looked upon Egypt as a province in a state of rebellion. He was helped by a large body of Spartan mercenaries, under the command of their own king Agesilaus, and his fleet was led by Chabrias the Athenian, who was fighting for the Egyptians against the command of his own state; for the Athenians and Spartans had lately changed sides, and the Athenians were now helping the Persians.

Aristoteles,
de Cura reif.
lib. ii.
In this hard struggle for freedom, when the treasure of Tachus, and the sums raised willingly by the priests, were spent, Chabrias persuaded the king to put a duty on the sale of corn; before this time all taxes, except the crown-rent on land, were unknown in Egypt.

When Tachus led his Greek mercenaries into Syria against the Diod. Sic. lib. xv. 92. Persians, the Egyptian troops set up Nectanebo II. as king; and Tachus fled to Persia, and even suffered himself to be named general of the invading army of Persians, against whom he was only a month before opposed. The Persian invasion was, however, stopt B.C. 358. by the death of Artaxerxes; but, nevertheless, Tachus and his twenty thousand Greeks overthrew the Egyptian army of one hundred thousand men, and regained the kingdom; but his death, which followed immediately, left Nectanebo king.

Nectanebo II. was for several years successful in keeping his throne against the armies of Persia, mainly by helping the Phenicians, who stood between Egypt and the invader. But most of the Greek states ranged themselves on the side of Persia; and though Nectanebo had twenty thousand Greeks in his pay, he was at last conquered by Ochus, and he fled with his treasures to Ethiopia.

On this, Egypt again became a Persian province. Ochus carefully levelled the fortifications of the cities, and carried with him into Persia a large weight of silver and gold, together with the sacred records from the temples, which however were afterwards sent back for a sum of money that was raised by the priests to ransom them. The country then remained for seventeen years under a Per- B.C. 333. sian satrap, till Alexander the Great, having conquered Darius in Asia Minor, instead of marching upon Persia, turned aside to the easier conquest of Egypt.

Alexander was stopt for some time before the little town of Gaza, Q. Curtius, lib. iv. where Batis, the brave governor, had the courage to close the gates against the Greek army. His impatience at being checked by so small a force was only equalled by his cruelty when he had overcome it; he tied Batis by the heels to his chariot, and dragged him round the walls of the city, as Achilles had dragged the body of Hector.

Arrian. lib. iii.

On the seventh day after leaving Gaza he reached Pelusium, the most easterly town in Egypt, after a march of one hundred and seventy miles along the coast of the Mediterranean, through a desert which forms the natural boundary of the country. The fleet kept close to the shore to carry the stores, as no fresh water is to be met with on the whole line of the march. The Egyptians did not even try to hide their joy at his approach: they were bending very unwillingly under the heavy and hated yoke of the Persians, who had long been looked upon as their natural enemies, and who in the pride of their success had added insults to the other evils of being governed by the satrap of a conqueror. They had not even gained the respect of the conquered by their warlike courage, for Egypt had in a great part been conquered and held by Greek mercenaries.

Q. Curtius,
lib. iv.

Arrian. lib. iii.

The Persian forces had been for the most part withdrawn from the country by Sabaces, the satrap of Egypt, to meet Alexander in Asia Minor, and had formed part of the army of Darius when he was beaten near the town of Issus on the coast of Cilicia. The garrisons were not strong enough to guard the towns left in their charge; the Greek fleet easily overpowered the Egyptian fleet in the harbour of Pelusium, and the town opened its gates to Alexander. Here he left a garrison, and ordering his fleet to meet him at Memphis, he marched the shortest way to Heliopolis, leaving the Nile on his right hand. All the towns on his march opened their gates to him. Mazakes, who had been left without an army as satrap of Egypt when Sabaces led the troops into Asia Minor, and who had heard of the shameful flight of Darius, of the death of Sabaces, and that Alexander was master of Phenicia, Syria, and the north of Arabia, had no choice but to yield up the fortified cities without a struggle. The Macedonian army crossed the Nile near Heliopolis, and then entered Memphis.

Memphis had long been the capital of all Egypt. In earlier ages, when the warlike virtues of the Thebans had made Egypt the greatest kingdom in the world, Memphis and the lowland corn-fields of the Delta paid tribute to Thebes; but, with the improvements in navigation, the cities on the coast rose in wealth; the navigation of the Red Sea, though always dangerous, became less dreaded, and Thebes lost the toll on the carrying trade of the Nile. Wealth alone, however, would not have given the sovereignty to Lower Egypt, had not the Greek mercenaries been at hand to fight for those who would pay them. The kings of Sais had guarded their thrones with Greek shields; and it was on the rash but praiseworthy attempt of Amasis to lessen the power of these mercenaries that they joined Cambyses, and Egypt became a Persian province.

In the struggles of the Egyptians to throw off the Persian yoke, we have seen little more than the Athenians and Spartans carrying on their old quarrels on the plains of the Delta; hence, when Alexander by his successes in Greece had put a stop to the feuds at home, the mercenaries of both parties flocked to his conquering standard, and he found himself on the throne of Upper and Lower Egypt without any struggle being made against him by the Egyptians.

Alexander's success as a general is almost thrown into the shade by his wisdom as a statesman. On reaching Memphis, his first care was to prove to the Egyptians that he was come to re-establish their ancient monarchy. He went in state to the temple of Apis, and sacrificed to the sacred bull, as the native kings had done at their coronations; and gained the good will of the crowd by games and music which were performed by skilful Greeks for their amusement.

Denon, plate 134.

But though the temple of Pthah at Memphis, in which the state ceremonies were performed, had risen in beauty and importance by the repeated additions of the later kings, who had fixed the seat of government in Lower Egypt, yet the Sun, or Amun-Ra, or Kneph-Ra, the god of Thebes, or Jupiter-Ammon as he was called by the Greeks, was the god under whose spreading wings Egypt had seen its proudest days. Every Egyptian king had called himself 'the son of the Sun;' those who had reigned at Thebes had boasted that they were 'beloved by Amun-Ra;' and when Alexander ordered the ancient titles to be used towards himself, he wished to lay his offerings in the temple of the god, and to be acknowledged by the priests as his son. As a reader of Homer, and the pupil of Aristotle, he must have wished to see the wonders of 'Egyptian Thebes,' the proper place for this ceremony; and it could only have been because, as a general, he had not time for a march of nine hundred miles, that he chose the nearer and less known temple of Kneph-Ra, in the Oasis of Ammon.

Arrian. lib. iii.

Accordingly, he floated down the river from Memphis to the sea, taking with him the light-armed troops and the royal band of knights-companions. When he reached Canopus, he sailed round the lake Marias and landed at Rhacotis, a small town on the spot where Alexandria now stands. Here he made no stay; but, as he passed through it, he must have seen at a glance, for he was never there a second time, that the place was formed by nature to be a great harbour, and that with a little help from art it would be the

Ammianus Marcellinus, lib. xxii.

port of all Egypt. He afterwards gave his orders to Dinocrates the architect to improve the harbour and to lay down the plan of his new city; and we shall hereafter see that the success of the undertaking proved the wisdom both of the statesman and of the builder.

From Rhacotis he marched along the coast to Parætonium, a Arrian. lib. iii. distance of about two hundred miles through the desert; and there, Q. Curtius, lib. iv. or on his way there, he was met by the ambassadors from Cyrene, who were sent with gifts to beg for peace, and to ask him to honour their city with a visit.

Cyrene, which together with four smaller cities was afterwards Justinus, lib. xiii. called the Pentapolis, was a Greek colony on the coast of the Mediterranean; it separated Carthage from Egypt, and was founded by Aristæus Battus, the son of Grinnus, king of the island of Theramenis. He had landed on the coast with his Dorian followers, Callimachus, Apoll. 89. and had driven back the people of the country, who were a wandering race of herdsmen called Marmaridæ, most likely part of Pausanias, lib. i. 7. the Arab race who had held Lower Egypt under the Shepherd kings.

Alexander graciously received the gifts of the Cyrenæans, and Q. Curtius, lib. iv. promised them his friendship, but could not spare the time to visit their city; and, without stopping, he marched southward to the oasis.

The oasis of Ammon is the most northerly of the three oases Arrian. lib. iii. of the Libyan desert. It is a green and shady valley in the midst of parched sand hills, refreshed by a deep spring of water, which, as it is always of nearly the same heat, seems cool in the hot hours of the day and warm when the air is cool at night. This little stream, after flowing through the valley, is lost in the dry sands. The spot was a halting-place for caravans passing from Parætonium to the next oasis, and it also carried on a small trade in sending to Lower Athenæus, lib. ii. 25. Egypt its valuable salt, which from the name of the place was called salt of Ammonia.

Here stood the temple of Amun-Ra. The figure of the god was Q. Curtius, lib. iv. that of a man having the head and horns of a ram; and the piety of the merchants, who left their treasures in the strong rooms of the temple while they rested their camels under the palm-trees, had loaded the statue with jewels. On holidays the priests carried the god about on a gilt barge, with silver dishes hanging from each side, while matrons and virgins followed singing his praises.

Alexander, on his approach with his army, was met by the chief priest of the temple, who, whether willing or unwilling, had no choice but to hail the conqueror of Egypt as ' the son of Amun-Ra ;' and having left his gifts in the temple, and gained the end of his journey, he returned the shortest way to Memphis.

Arrian. lib. iii.

Alexander has been much laughed at by the Greeks for calling himself the son of Ammon; but it should be remembered that it was only among people who worshipped and built temples to their kings that he, for reasons of state, called himself a god; that he never was guilty of the folly of claiming such honours in Greece, or of his Greek soldiers; and that among his friends he always allowed his divinity to be made the subject of a good-humoured joke.

Plutarch.
in Alexand.

At Memphis he received the ambassadors that came from Greece to wish him joy of his success; he reviewed his troops, and gave out his plans for the government of his new kingdom ; he divided the country into two nomarchies or judgeships, and to fill these two offices of nomarchs or chief judges, the highest civil offices in the kingdom, he chose Doloaspis and Pet-isis, two Egyptians. Their duty was to watch over the due administration of justice, one in Upper and the other in Lower Egypt, and perhaps to hear appeals from the lower judges.

Arrian. lib. iii.

He left the garrisons in the command of his own Greek generals; Pantaleon commanded the counts, or knights-companions, who garrisoned Memphis, and Polemon was governor of Pelusium.

These were the chief fortresses in the kingdom: Memphis over-looked the Delta, the navigation of the river, and the pass to Upper Egypt; Pelusium was the harbour for the ships of war, and the frontier town on the only side on which Egypt could be attacked. The other cities were given to other governors; Licidas com-manded the mercenaries, Eugnostus was secretary, while Æschylus and Ephippus were left as overlookers, or perhaps, in the language of modern governments, as civil commissioners. Orders were given to all these generals that justice was to be administered by the Egyptian nomarchs according to the common law, or ancient cus-toms of the land. Pet-isis, however, either never entered upon his office or soon quitted it, and Doloaspis was left nomarch of all Egypt.

This is perhaps the earliest instance that history has recorded, of a conqueror governing a province according to its own laws, and upholding the religion of the conquered as the established religion of the state; and the length of time that the Græco-Egyptian mo-narchy lasted, and the splendour with which it shone, prove the wisdom and humanity of the founder. This example has been copied, with equal success, in our own colonial and Indian govern-ments; but we do not know whether Alexander had any such ex-ample to guide his views, or whether his own good sense pointed out to him the folly of those who wished to make a people not only open their gates to the garrisons, but their minds to the civil and religious opinions of the conquerors. At any rate, the highest meed of praise is due to the statesman, whoever he may have been, who first taught the world this lesson of statesmanlike wisdom and religious humanity.

Alexander did not stay longer than was necessary to give these orders. He had found time to talk with Psammo, the philosopher of the greatest name then in Memphis; but, though the buildings

Plutarch. in Alexandro.

of Upper Egypt were unvisited, he hastened towards the Euphrates to meet Darius. In his absence Egypt remained quiet and happy; and though Cleomenes, who was at the head of the taxes, seems in his zeal to have forgotten the mild feelings which guided his master, yet upon the whole, after the galling yoke of the Persians, the Egyptians must have felt grateful for the blessings of justice and good government.

Aristoteles, de Cura reif. lib. ii. One summer, when the harvest had been less plentiful than usual, Cleomenes forbad the export of corn, which was a large part of the trade of Egypt. On this, the heads of the provinces sent to him in alarm, to say that they should not be able to get in the usual amount of tribute: he therefore allowed the export as usual, but raised the duty; by which he received a larger revenue at the very time that the landholders were suffering from a smaller crop.

At another time, when passing along the Nile in his barge, in the Thebaid, he was wrecked, and one of his children bitten by a crocodile. On this plea, he called together the priests, probably of Crocodilopolis, where this animal was held sacred, and told them. that he was going to revenge himself upon the crocodiles by having them all caught and killed; and he was only bought off from carrying his threat into execution by the priests giving him all the treasure which they could get together.

Alexander had left orders that the great market should be moved from Canopus to his new city of Alexandria, as soon as it should be ready to receive it. As the building went forward, the priests and rich traders of Canopus, in alarm at losing the advantages of their port, gave Cleomenes a large sum of money for leave to keep their market. This sum he took, and when the building at Alexandria was finished he again came to Canopus, and because the traders would not or could not raise a second and larger sum, he carried Alexander's orders into execution, and closed the market of their city.

But instances, such as these, of a public officer making use of dishonest means to raise the amount of revenue which it was his duty to collect, might, unfortunately, be found even in countries which were for the most part enjoying the blessings of wise laws and good government; and it is not probable that, while Alexander was with the army in Persia, the acts of fraud and wrong should have been fewer in his own kingdom of Macedonia.

The dishonesty of Cleomenes was indeed equally shown toward the Macedonians, by his wish to cheat the troops out of part of their pay. The pay of the soldiers was due on the first day of each month, but on that day he took care to be out of the way, and the soldiers were paid a few days later; and by doing the same on each following month, he at length changed the pay-day to the last day of the month, and cheated the army of a month's pay.

A somatophylax, in the Macedonian army, was no doubt at first, as the word means, one of the officers who had to answer for the safety of the king's person—perhaps, in modern language, a colonel in the body-guards or household troops: but as, in unmixed monarchies, the faithful officer who was nearest the king's person, to whose watchfulness he trusted in the hour of danger, often found himself the king's adviser in matters of state, so, in the time of Alexander, the title of somatophylax was given to those generals on whose wisdom the king chiefly leant, and by whose advice he was usually guided. Among these, and foremost in Alexander's love and esteem, was Ptolemy the son of Lagus.

Arrian.
lib. iii.

Philip, the father of Alexander, had given Arsinoë, one of his relations, in marriage to Lagus; and her eldest son Ptolemy, born soon after the marriage, was always thought to be the king's son,

Pausanias,
lib. i. 6.

though never so acknowledged. He was put into the highest offices by Philip, without raising in Alexander's mind the distrust which might have been felt if Ptolemy had boasted that he was the elder brother. He had earned the good opinion of Alexander by his military successes in Asia, and had gained his gratitude by saving his life when he was in danger among the Oxydracæ, near the river Indus; and moreover, Alexander looked up to him as the historian whose literary powers and knowledge of military tactics were to hand down to the wonder of future ages those conquests of which he was an eye-witness.

Q. Curtius, lib. x. Justinus, lib. xiii. B.C. 324.

Alexander's victories over Darius, and march to the river Indus, are no part of this history: it is enough to say that he died at Babylon, eight years after he had entered Egypt; and his half-brother Philip Arridæus, a weak-minded unambitious young man, was declared by the generals assembled at Babylon to be his successor. His royal blood united more voices in the army in his favour than the warlike and statesmanlike character of any one of the rival generals. They were forced to be content with dividing the provinces between them; some hoping to govern by their power over the weak mind of Arridæus, and others secretly meaning to make themselves independent.

In this weighty matter, Ptolemy showed the wisdom and judgement which had already gained him his high character. Though his military rank and skill were equal to those of any one of the generals of Alexander, and his claim by birth perhaps equal to that of Arridæus, he was not one of those who had aimed at the throne; nor had he even aimed at the second place, but left to Perdiccas the regency, with the care of the king's person, in whose name that ambitious general vainly hoped to govern the whole of Alexander's conquests. But Ptolemy, more wisely measuring his strength with the several tasks, chose the province of Egypt, the province which was of all others, from its insulated position, the easiest to be held as an independent kingdom against the power of Perdiccas : and, when Egypt was given to Ptolemy by the council of generals, Cleomenes was at the same time and by the same power made second in command, and he governed Egypt for one year before Ptolemy's arrival.

Arrian.
ap. Photium,
lib. x.

THE FAMILY OF THE LAGIDÆ.

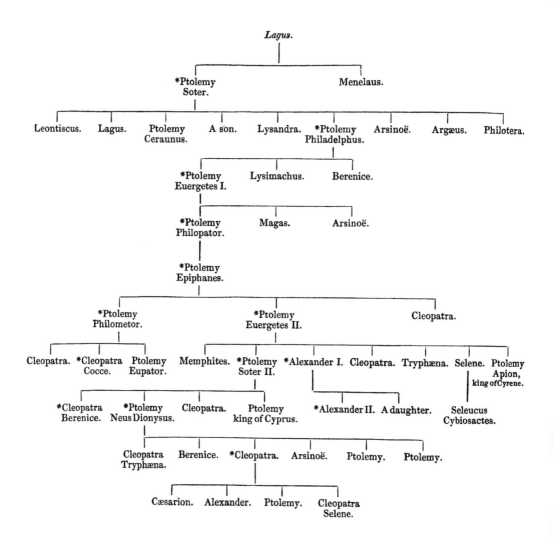

PTOLEMY THE SON OF LAGUS,

OR PTOLEMY SOTER.

WHENEVER a man of ambition aims at raising himself by means B.C. 322. of industry and ability to a higher rank in the world than that in which he was born, if he seeks to throw off his family and to break those ties by which he fancies that he is held back, the opinion of the world as certainly chains him to the load that he wishes to rise from. Any body with less good sense and knowledge of mankind than Ptolemy would have called himself the natural son of Philip Amyntas, and would have wished his relationship with Lagus to have been forgotten; but we may be sure that in that case the name of Lagus would have been thrown at him as a reproach, and he more wisely took it as his title; instead of being ashamed of his father's name he ennobled it, and took care that his children and his children's children should be proud of being of the family of the Lagidæ.

He was one of those who, at the death of Alexander, had raised Pausanias, lib. i. 6. their voices against giving the whole of the conquered countries to one king; he had wished that they should have been shared equally among the generals as independent kingdoms; but in this he was overruled, and he accepted his government as the lieutenant of Philip Arridæus, though no doubt with the fixed purpose of making Egypt an independent kingdom. On reaching Memphis, the seat of his government, his whole thoughts were turned toward strengthening himself against Perdiccas, who hoped to be obeyed, in the name of his young and weak-minded king, by all his fellow generals.

The Greek and foreign mercenaries, of which the army of Alexander was made up, and who were faithful to his memory and to his family, had little to guide them in the choice of which leader they should follow to his distant province, beside the thought of where they should be best treated; and Ptolemy's high character for wisdom, generosity, and warlike skill had gained many friends for him among the officers: they saw that the wealth of Egypt would put it in his power to reward those whose services were valuable to him; and hence crowds flocked to his standard.

On reaching their provinces, the Greek soldiers, proud of their conquests and of their late king, always called themselves Macedonians; they pleased themselves with the thought that the whole of the conquered countries were still governed by the brother of Alexander; and no one of his generals was unwise enough, in his wildest thoughts of ambition—whether aiming like Ptolemy at founding a kingdom, or like Perdiccas at the government of the world,—to throw off the title of lieutenant to Philip Arridæus, and to forfeit the love of the Macedonian soldiers and his best claim to their loyalty.

The first act of Ptolemy was to put to death Cleomenes, who had been made receiver-general of the taxes by Alexander, and who had afterwards been made sub-governor of Egypt by the same council of generals which had made Ptolemy governor. This may easily have been called for by the dishonesty and crooked dealing which Cleomenes had been guilty of in getting in the taxes; and while the whole tenor of Ptolemy's life would disprove the charge, we must not accuse him of being led to this deed because he might have looked upon Cleomenes as the friend of Perdiccas, or because he could not trust him in his plans for making himself king of Egypt.

The first addition which he made to his kingdom was the little state of Cyrene and its sister cities, which had before asked for the friendship of Alexander, but was still in name a free state. It was then being torn to pieces by the struggles of two parties for power, which ended in an appeal to arms; and the nobles were driven out to seek for help from Ptolemy. This was readily granted: he led them back in triumph into their city, and Cyrene became the prize of the conquering umpire.

Diod. Sic. lib. xviii.

In the second year after the death of Alexander, the funeral train set out from Babylon to carry the body of the conqueror to its place of burial. This sacred charge had been given to a general named Arridæus, who followed the chariot with a strong band of soldiers. In every city through which the funeral passed the people came out in crowds to gaze upon the dazzling show, and to pay their last homage to the embalmed body of their king.

B.C. 321.

Perdiccas had given orders that it should be carried to Æga in Macedonia, the burial-place of Philip and his forefathers; for such was the love borne by the soldiers to Alexander, even after his death, that it was thought that the city which should have the honour of being his last resting-place would be the seat of government for the whole of his wide conquests.

Pausanias, lib. i. 6; and Arrian. ap. Photium, lib. x.

But Ptolemy had gained over Arridæus to favour his ambitious views; and when the funeral reached Syria he met it with an army which he led out of Egypt to honour and to guard the sacred prize. He then gave out that the body was to be buried in the oasis of Ammon, in the temple of the god who had acknowledged Alexander as his son; but, when the joint armies reached Memphis, they left it there, till the new city of Alexandria should be ready to re-

Diod. Sic. lib. xviii.

ceive it; and we shall soon see that Ptolemy, who never forgot to reward any one who had been of use to him, gave to Arridæus the earliest and greatest gift that he had in his power to give.

Perdiccas, who, in the death of Cleomenes and the seizure of the body of Alexander, had seen quite enough proof that Ptolemy, though he was too wise to take the name of king, had in reality grasped the power, now led the Macedonian army against Egypt, to enforce obedience and to punish the rebellious lieutenant. He carried with him the two kings, Philip Arridæus and the infant Alexander Ægus, the son of Alexander the Great born after his father's death, both to ornament his army and to prove his right to issue orders over the provinces. At Pelusium he was met by Ptolemy, who had strengthened all his cities, and had left garrisons in them; and, when he laid siege to a small fortress near Pelusium, Ptolemy forced him to withdraw his troops and to retire to his camp. At night, however, he left his trenches without any noise, and marched hastily towards Memphis, leaving the garrisoned towns in his rear.

In this bold and as it would seem rash step, Perdiccas was badly supported by his generals. He was stern and overbearing in his manner; he never asked advice from a council of war; his highest officers were kept in the dark about tomorrow's march; he wished to be obeyed, without caring to be loved. Ptolemy, on the other hand, was just and mild to every body; he always sought the advice of his generals, and listened to them as his equals: he was beloved alike by officers and soldiers. Hence when Perdiccas, in his attempt to cross the Nile near Memphis, received a check from the army of Ptolemy, whole bodies of men, headed by their generals, left their ranks and went over to the Egyptian army; and among them Python, a general who had held the same rank under

Pausanias, lib. i. 6.

Diod. Sic. lib. xviii.

Alexander as Perdiccas himself, and who would no longer put up with his haughty commands. On this the disorder spread through the whole army, and Perdiccas soon fell by the hand of one of his own soldiers.

On the death of their leader, all cause of war ceased. Ptolemy sent food into the camp of the invading army, which then asked for orders from him who the day before had been their enemy. The princes, Philip Arridæus and the young Alexander, both fell into his hands; and he might then, as guardian, in their name have sent his orders over the whole of Alexander's conquests. But, by grasping at what was clearly out of his reach, he would have lost more friends and power than he would have gained; and when the Macedonian phalanx, whose voice was law to the rest of the army, asked his advice in the choice of a guardian for the two princes, he recommended to them Python and Arridæus—Python, who had just joined him, and had been the cause of the rout of the Macedonian army, and Arridæus, who had given up to him the body of Alexander.

The Macedonian army, accordingly, chose Python and Arridæus as guardians, and as rulers with unlimited power over the whole of Alexander's conquests; but, though none of the Greek generals who now held Asia Minor, Syria, Babylonia, Thrace, or Egypt, dared to acknowledge it to the soldiers, yet in reality the power of the guardians was limited to the little kingdom of Macedonia. With the death of Perdiccas, and the withdrawal of his army, Phenicia and Cœlo-Syria were left unguarded, and almost without a master; and Ptolemy, who had before been kept back by his wise forethought rather than by the moderation of his views, sent an army under the command of Nicanor to conquer those countries. Jerusalem was the only place that held out against the Egyptian

Josephus,
contra
Apionem.
army; but Nicanor, seeing that on every seventh day the garrison withdrew from the walls, chose that day for the assault, and gained the city.

In the earlier times of Egyptian history, when navigation was less easy and seas separated kingdoms instead of joining them, the Thebaid enjoyed, under the Coptic kings, the trading wealth which followed the stream of its great river, the longest piece of inland navigation then known; but, with the improvement in navigation and ship-building, countries began to feel their strength in the timber of their forests and the number of their harbours; and, as timber and sea-coast were equally unknown in the Thebaid, that country fell as Lower Egypt rose; the wealth which before centred in Thebes was then found in the ports of the Delta, where the barges of the Nile met the ships of the Mediterranean. What used to be Egypt was an inland kingdom, bounded by the desert; but Egypt under Ptolemy was a country on the sea-coast; and on the conquest of Phenicia and Cœlo-Syria he was master of the forests of Lebanon and Antilibanus, and stretched his coast from Cyrene to Antioch, a distance of twelve hundred miles.

The wise and mild plans which were laid down by Alexander for the government of Egypt, when a province, were easily followed by Ptolemy when it became his own kingdom. The Macedonian soldiers lived in their garrisons or in Alexandria under the Greek laws; while the Egyptian laws were administered by their own priests, who were upheld in all the rights of their order and in their freedom from land-tax. The temples of Pthah, of Amun-Ra, and the other gods of the country were not only kept open but repaired and built at the cost of the king; the religion of the people and not the religion of the rulers was made the established religion of Diod. Sic.
lib. i. 84. the state. On the death of the god Apis, the sacred bull of Mem-

phis, the chief of the animals which were kept and fed at the cost of the several cities, and who had died of old age soon after Ptolemy came to Egypt, he spent the sum of fifty talents or eight thousand five hundred pounds on its funeral: and the priests, who had not forgotten that Cambyses their former conqueror had wounded the Apis of his day with his own sword, must have been highly pleased with this mark of his care for them.

The Egyptians, who during the two last centuries had sometimes had their temples plundered and their trade crushed by the grasping tyranny of the Persian satraps, and had at other times been almost as much hurt by their own vain struggles for freedom, now found themselves in the quiet enjoyment of equal laws, with a prosperity which promised soon to equal that of the reigns of Necho or Amasis.

It is true that they had not regained their independence and political liberty, and that they only enjoyed their civil rights during the pleasure of a Greek autocrat; but then it is to be remembered that the native rulers with whom Ptolemy was compared were the kings of Lower Egypt, who like himself were surrounded by Greek mercenaries, and who never rested their power on the broad base of national pride and love of country; and that nobody could have hoped to see a Theban king arise to bring back the days of Thothmosis and Rameses. Thebes was every day sinking in wealth and strength, and its race of hereditary soldiers, proud in the recollection of former glory, who had after centuries of struggles been forced to receive laws from Memphis, perhaps obeyed a Greek conqueror with less pain than they had their own vassals of Lower Egypt.

The building of the city of Alexandria, which was begun before the death of Alexander, was carried on briskly by Ptolemy, though many of the public works were only finished in the reign of his son.

Strabo,
lib. xvii.

The two main streets crossed one another at right angles in the middle of the city, which was thirty stadia or three miles long, and seven stadia broad; and the whole of the streets were wide enough for carriages. In front of the city is a long narrow island named Pharos, which in the piercing mind of Alexander only needed a little help from art to become the breakwater of a large harbour. Accordingly one end of the island of Pharos was joined to the main land by a stone mole seven stadia or nearly three quarters of a mile long, which from its length was called the Heptastadium. There were two breaks in the mole to let the water pass, without which perhaps the harbour might have become blocked up with sand; and bridges were thrown over these two passages, while the mouth of the harbour was between the main land and the other end of the island. Most of the public buildings of the city fronted the harbour: among these were the royal docks for building the ships of war; the Posideion or temple of Neptune, which naturally had a place in a sea-port town, where the Greek sailors might offer up their vows on setting sail, or perform them on their safe return from a long voyage; and the Emporium or exchange, which had, by the favour of its founder, gained the privileges which before belonged to the city of Canopus. There also stood the burial-place for the Greek kings of Egypt, which was named the Soma, because it held ' the body,' as that of Alexander was from its importance called.

On the other side of the Heptastadium, and on the outside of the city, were some more docks, and a ship-canal into the lake Mareotis; the Necropolis or public burial-place for the city; also a theatre, an amphitheatre, a gymnasium with a large *stoa* or portico, a stadium in which games were celebrated every fifth year, a hall of justice, public groves or gardens, and a hippodrome for chariot races.

On the outside of the city, with these buildings, was the temple of Serapis, the god whose worship became so popular in the later ages of the Roman empire. The Egyptian god Osiris was at the same time the bearded Bacchus of the Greeks, the conqueror of India beyond the Ganges, and the god of the lower regions, who sat as judge while the actions of the dead were weighed before him in a pair of scales. He seems about this time to have been divided into two persons; one of these was named Pthah-sokar Osiris, and the other Apis-Osiris, or Osiri-Apis. The latter, who was called Serapis by the Greeks, was in this division of the persons made the husband of Isis and the judge of the dead; and it may have been for this reason that his temple was always on the outside of the city walls with the public burial-place. He is known by his having, beside the whip and crosier which are the two sceptres of Osiris, a bull's head, which shows his connection with Apis. Osiris was also the god from whom the native kings traced their pedigree, and as, after the favour now shown to the priests, the Ptolemies were no longer to be counted as foreign conquerors, a new god was added to the mythology, who was given as another son to Osiris, and named Macedon, from whom the Macedonian kings were said to have sprung, and they were thus brought into the religion of the people.

Egypt. Inscrip. plate 4.

Diod. Sic. lib. i. 18.

But among the public buildings of Alexandria which were planned in the enlarged mind of Ptolemy, the one which chiefly calls for our notice, the one indeed to which the city owes its fairest fame, is the Museum or college of philosophy. Its chief room was a great hall, which was used as a lecture-room and common dining-room; it had a covered walk or portico all round the outside, and

Strabo, lib. xvii.

there was an *exhedra* or seat on which the philosophers sometimes
sat in the open air. The professors or fellows of the college were
supported by a public income. Ptolemy was himself an author;
his history of the wars of Alexander was highly praised by Arrian,
in whose pages we now read much of it; his love of art was shown
in the buildings of Alexandria; and those agreeable manners and
that habit of rewarding skill and knowledge wherever he could find
them, which had already brought to his army many of the bravest
of Alexander's soldiers, were now equally successful in bringing to
his court such painters and sculptors, such poets, historians, and
mathematicians, as soon made the Museum of Alexandria one of
the brightest spots in the known world. The arts and letters, which
he then planted, did not perhaps bear their richest fruit till the
reign of his son, but they took such good root that they continued
to flourish under the last of his successors, unchoked by the vices
and follies by which they were then surrounded.

Pliny,
lib. xiii. 21.

In return for the literature which Greece then gave to Egypt,
she gained the knowledge of papyrus. Before that time books had
been written on linen, wax, bark, or the leaves of trees; and public
records on stone, brass, or lead: but the knowledge of papyrus was
felt by all men of letters like the invention of printing in modern
Europe; books were then known by many for the first time, and
very little else was afterwards used in Greece or Rome; for when
parchment was made about two centuries later, it was too costly
to be used as long as papyrus was within reach.

While Egypt under Ptolemy was thus enjoying the advantages
of its insulated position, and was thereby at leisure to cultivate
the arts of peace, the other provinces had been harrassed by the
unceasing wars of the several generals of Alexander, who were
aiming like Ptolemy at raising their own power. Many changes

had taken place among them in the short space of eight years which had passed since the death of Alexander. Philip Arridæus, in whose name the provinces had been governed, had been put to death; Antigonus was master of Asia Minor, with a kingdom more powerful though not so easily guarded as Egypt; Cassander held Macedonia, and had the care of the young Alexander Ægus, who was then called the heir to the whole of his father's wide conquests, and whose life, like that of Arridæus, was soon to end with his minority; Lysimachus was trying to form a kingdom in Thrace; and Seleucus had for a short time held Babylonia.

With the wars which brought about these changes Ptolemy had no part, beyond being once or twice called upon to send troops to guard his province of Cœlo-Syria. But Antigonus, in his ambitious efforts to establish his power over the whole of the provinces, had by force or treachery driven Seleucus out of Babylon, who fled to Egypt for safety, where Ptolemy received him with the kindness and good policy which had before gained so many friends. No arguments of Seleucus were wanting to persuade him that Antigonus was aiming at universal conquest, and that his next attack would be upon Egypt. He therefore sent ambassadors to Cassander and Lysimachus, who readily joined him against the common enemy.

The large fleet and army which Antigonus got together for the invasion of Egypt proved his opinion of the strength and skill of Ptolemy. All Syria, except one or two cities, laid down its arms before him on his approach. But he found that the whole of the fleet had been already removed to the ports of Egypt, and he ordered Phenicia to furnish him with eight thousand ship-builders and carpenters, to build gallies from the forests of Lebanon and Antilibanus, and ordered Syria to send four hundred and fifty thousand medimni or nearly three millions of bushels of wheat, for the

use of his army within the year. By these means he raised his fleet
to two hundred and forty-three long gallies or ships of war.

B.C. 313. Ptolemy was called off for a short time from the war in Syria by
a rising in Cyrene. The Cyrenæans had taken arms and were be-
sieging the Egyptian, or as they would have called themselves the
Macedonian garrison, who had shut themselves up in the citadel.
He at first sent messengers to order the Cyrenæans to return to
their duty; but his orders were not listened to; the rebels no doubt
thought themselves safe, as his armies seemed more wanted on the
eastern frontier; his messengers were put to death, and the siege
of the citadel pushed forward with all possible speed. On this he
sent a large land force, followed by a fleet, in order to crush the
revolt at a single blow, and the ring-leaders were brought to Alexandria in chains.

When this trouble at home was put an end to, Ptolemy crossed
over to Cyprus, to punish the kings of the little states on that
island for having joined 'Antigonus. His force was so large that
he met with no resistance; he made Nicocreon governor of the
whole island, and seized the revenues of the banished kings.

The large and safe harbours of Cyprus gave a great value to this
island in the naval warfare between Egypt, Phenicia, and Asia
Arrian. lib. i. Minor. Alexander had given it as his opinion that the command
of the sea went with the island of Cyprus; when he held Asia
Minor he called Cyprus the key to Egypt, and with still greater
reason might Ptolemy, looking from Egypt, think that island the
key to Phenicia. Cyprus was also famous for its manufacture of
Plutarch. armour. Demetrius the son of Antigonus, if we may believe Plu-
Vit. Demet. tarch, had a coat of mail made of Cyprian adamant, which was so
hard that no dart, even when thrown by a machine, could make a
dent in it. The early writers have left us no account of when the

art of making steel was first learnt, but, as the furnaces were heated with wood, the iron must often have been hardened into steel by the mere accident of the air being shut out, and it seems difficult to believe that the armour of Demetrius could have been made of any thing else. If this be granted it would carry back the use of steel to some centuries earlier, as the Cyprian breast-plate in which Agamemnon fought against Troy may also have been made of steel. Iliad, xi. 20.

From Cyprus, Ptolemy landed with his army in Upper Syria, as the northern part of that country was called, while the part nearer to Palestine was called Cœlo-Syria. Here he took the towns of Posideion and Potami-Caron, and then marching hastily into Asia Minor he took Mallus a city of Cilicia. Having rewarded his soldiers with the booty there taken, he again embarked aud returned to Alexandria. Diod. Sic. lib. xix.

This inroad seems to have been meant to draw off the enemy from Cœlo-Syria, and it had the wished-for effect; for Demetrius, who commanded the forces of his father Antigonus in that quarter, marched northward to the relief of Cilicia, but he did not arrive there till Ptolemy's fleet was already under sail for Egypt.

Ptolemy, on reaching Alexandria, set his army in motion towards Pelusium, on its way to Palestine. His forces were eighteen thousand foot and four thousand horse, part Macedonians, as the Greeks living in Egypt were always called, and part mercenaries, followed by a crowd of Egyptians, of whom some were armed for battle and some were to take care of the baggage.

There are in all ages some nations who are so much before others in warlike skill and courage, that no inequality of numbers can make up for it. Not that one Greek could overcome ten barbarians, but that a body of Greeks, if large enough to make an army, with a centre, wings, heavy-armed, light-armed, and cavalry, would never think it worth while to count the crowd of barbarians that might be led against them. The number wanted to make an army has changed with the art of war: in modern Europe it must be much larger, perhaps ten times what was needed before gunpowder was used; but we may quote the retreat of the ten thousand under Xenophon to prove that that number was enough with the Greeks. When Greeks met Greeks it is probable that the larger army would conquer, but ten thousand Greeks would beat any number of barbarians. This will help us to understand the low state of discipline among the native Egyptians under Ptolemy; when measuring his strength against Demetrius, he took no account of their number, —he had twenty-two thousand Greeks and a crowd of Egyptians.

Diod. Sic.
lib. xix.
He was met at Gaza by the young Demetrius with an army of eleven thousand foot and twenty-three hundred horse, followed by forty-three elephants, and a body of light-armed barbarians, who, like the Egyptians in the army of Ptolemy, were not counted. But the youthful courage of Demetrius was no match for the cool skill and larger army of Ptolemy; the elephants were easily stopt by iron hurdles, and the Egyptian army after gaining a complete victory entered Gaza, while Demetrius fled to Azotus. Ptolemy, who might have thought in this almost civil strife that as much was to be gained by the arts of friendship as by war, not only gave leave to the conquered army to bury their dead, but sent back the whole of the royal baggage which had fallen into his hands, and also those personal friends of Demetrius who were found among the prisoners; that is to say, all those who were sorry to be taken, as the larger part of these Greek armies were equally ready to fight on either side.

By this victory the whole of Phenicia was again joined to Egypt, and Seleucus regained Babylonia; where, by following the example of Ptolemy in his good treatment of the people, and in leaving them their own laws and religion, he founded a monarchy, and gave his name to a race of kings which rivalled even the Lagidæ.

When Antigonus, who was in Phrygia, on the other side of his kingdom, heard that his son Demetrius had been beaten at Gaza, he marched with all his forces to give battle to Ptolemy. He soon crossed Mount Taurus, the lofty range which divides Asia Minor from Syria and Mesopotamia, and joined his camp to that of his son in Upper Syria. But Ptolemy had gone through life without ever making a hazardous move—not indeed without ever suffering a loss, but without ever fighting a battle when its loss would have ruined him, and he did not choose to risk his kingdom against the far larger forces of Antigonus. By the advice of his council of generals, he levelled the fortifications of Aca, Joppa, Samaria, and Gaza, and withdrew the whole of his forces and treasure into Egypt, leaving the desert between himself and the army of Antigonus.

Antigonus could not safely attempt to march through the desert in the face of Ptolemy's army. He had therefore, first, either to conquer or gain the friendship of the Nabatæans, a warlike race of Arabs who held the north of Arabia; and then he might march by Petra, Mount Sinai, and the coast of the Red Sea, without being in want of water for his army. The Nabatæans professed neutrality between these two contending powers; but the mild temper of Ptolemy had so far gained their friendship that the haughty Antigonus, though he did not refuse their pledges of peace, secretly made up his mind to conquer them.

Petra, the city of the Nabatæans, is in a narrow rocky valley between high mountains, with an approach between steep overhanging rocks, so that a handful of men could guard it against the largest army. A large stream of water within the valley, in addi-

Pliny, lib. vi. 32. Laborde's Travels.

tion to the strength of the place, made it a favourite resting-place
for caravans, which, whether they were coming from Tyre or Jerusalem, were forced to pass through this city in their way to the
Incense Country of Arabia Felix, or to the Elanitic Gulf of the Red
Sea. These warlike Arabs seem to have received a toll from the
caravans, and they held their rocky fastness unconquered by the
great nations which surrounded them. Their temples and houses
were cut out of the live rock, and hence the city was by the Greeks
named Petra, from which the country was sometimes called Arabia
Petræa.

Diod. Sic.
lib. xix. Antigonus heard that the Nabatæans had left Petra less guarded
than usual, and had gone to a neighbouring fair, probably to meet
a caravan from the south, and to receive spices in exchange for the
woollen goods from Tyre. He therefore sent forward four thousand light-armed foot and six hundred horse, who overpowered the
guard and seized the city. The Arabs, when they heard of what had
happened, returned in the night, surrounded the place, came upon
the Greeks from above, by paths known only to themselves,
and overcame them with such slaughter, that out of the four thousand six hundred men only fifty returned to Antigonus to tell the
tale.

The Nabatæans then sent to Antigonus to complain of this attack
upon Petra. He endeavoured to put them off their guard by dis-
owning the acts of his general: he sent them home with promises
of peace, and at the same time sent forward his son Demetrius,
with four thousand horse and four thousand foot, to take revenge
upon them and again seize their city. But the Arabs were this
time upon their guard; the nature of the place was as unfavourable
to the Greek arms and warfare as it was favourable to the Arabs;
and these eight thousand men, the flower of the army, under the

brave Demetrius, were unable to force their way through the narrow pass into the city.

Had Antigonus been master of the sea, he might perhaps have
marched through the desert, along the coast of the Mediterranean,
to Pelusium, with his fleet to wait upon his army, as Perdiccas had
done. But without this, the only way that he could enter Egypt
was through Petra, along the same path by which the Jews under
Moses had come out; and the stop thus put upon the invasion of
Egypt by this little city shows us the strength of Ptolemy's eastern
frontier. Antigonus then led his army northward, leaving Egypt
unattacked.

This was followed by a treaty of peace between these generals, B.C. 310.
by which it was agreed that each should keep the country that he
then held; that Cassander should govern Macedonia until Alexander Ægus, the son of Alexander the Great, should be of age; that
Lysimachus should keep Thrace, Ptolemy Egypt, and Antigonus
Asia Minor; and each wishing to be looked upon as the friend of
the soldiers by whom his power was upheld and the whole of these
wide conquests kept in awe, added the very unnecessary article, that
the Greeks living in each of these countries should be governed
according to their own laws.

All the provinces held by these generals became more or less
Greek kingdoms, yet in no one did so many Greeks settle as in
Lower Egypt. Though the rest of Egypt was governed by Egyptian laws and judges, the city of Alexandria was under Macedonian
law. In that city no Egyptian could live without feeling himself
of a conquered race: he was not admitted, except by an especial
favour, to the privileges of Macedonian citizenship; while they were
at once granted to every Greek, and soon to every Jew, who would
settle there. Hence, although the city was crowded with Egyptians

who kept the shops and filled the lower ranks, and though the Greeks must very much have married Egyptian wives, yet it was long before these mixed races were melted down into Egyptians.

Vocab. Hier. No. 722.
The same hieroglyphical word stood for Greek and for Lower-Egyptian; Lycophron seems to speak of the Egyptian nation under Polybius, lib. xv. the name of Macedonians; and whenever, during the reigns of the Ptolemies, the citizens of the capital of Egypt met in public as-sembly, they were addressed, 'Ye men of Macedonia.'

Diod. Sic. lib. xix.
By this treaty Ptolemy, in the thirteenth year after the death of Alexander, was left undisputed master of Egypt. During these years he had not only gained the love of the Egyptians and Alex-andrians by his wise and just government, but had won their respect as a general by the skill with which he had kept the war at a distance. He had lost and won battles at sea, in Syria, in Asia Minor, and in the island of Cyprus; but, since Perdiccas marched against him before he had a force to defend himself with, no foreign army had been seen upon the banks of the Nile.

It was under the government of Ptolemy that the wonders of Upper Egypt were first seen by any Greeks who had a love of know-ledge and enough of literature to examine carefully and to describe what they saw. Loose and highly-coloured accounts of the wealth of Thebes had reached Greece even before the time of Homer, and again through Herodotus and other travellers in the Delta; but nothing was certainly known of it till it was visited by Hecatæus of Abdera.

lib. xvii. 5.

lib. ii. 47.

lib. i. 46.
Hecatæus had been an officer in the army of Alexander, and he afterwards joined himself to Ptolemy; but he is best known as an author. Among other works, he wrote a history of the Hyperbo-rean or northern nations, and also a history or rather a descrip-tion of Egypt, part of which we now read in the pages of Diodorus

Siculus. When he travelled in Upper Egypt, Thebes, though still a populous city, was more thought of by the antiquary than by the statesman. Its wealth however was still great; and when, under Diod. Sic. lib. i. the just government of Ptolemy, it was no longer necessary for the priests to hide their treasures, it was found that the temples still held the very large sum of three hundred talents of gold, and two thousand three hundred talents of silver, or above one million sterling, which had escaped the plundering hands of the Persian satraps.

Many of the Theban tombs, which are sets of rooms tunnelled into the hills on the Libyan side of the Nile, had even then been opened to gratify the curiosity of the learned or the greediness of the conqueror. Forty-seven royal tombs were mentioned in the records of the priests, of which the entrances had been covered up with earth and hidden in the sloping sides of the hills, in the hope that they might remain undisturbed and unplundered, and might keep safe the embalmed bodies of the kings, till they should rise again at the end of the world; and seventeen of these had already been found out and broken open. Hecatæus was told that the other tombs had been before destroyed, and we owe it perhaps to this mistake that they have remained unopened for more than two thousand years longer, to reward the searches of modern travellers, and to unfold the history of their builders.

The Memnonium, the great palace of Rameses II., was then standing; and though it had been plundered by the Persians the building itself was unhurt. Its massive walls had scarcely felt the wear of the centuries which had rolled over them. Hecatæus measured its rooms, its courtyards, and its avenue of sphinxes, and by his measurements we can now distinguish its ruins from those of the other palaces of Thebes.

Diod. Sic.
lib. i.
One of its rooms, perhaps after the days of its builder, had been fitted up as a library, and held the histories and records of the priests; but the golden zodiac or circle, on which were engraved the days of the year, with the heliacal rising and setting of the stars, by which each day was known, had been taken away by Cambyses. Hecatæus also saw the three other palace-temples of Thebes, which we now call by the names of the villages in which they stand; namely, of Luxor, of Karnak, and of Medinet Abu.

If Ptolemy did not make his government as much feared by the half-armed Ethiopians as it was by the well-disciplined Europeans, it must have been because the Thebans wished to guard their own frontier rather than because his troops were always wanted against a more powerful enemy; but the inroads of the Ethiopians were so far from being checked that the country to the south of Thebes was unsafe for travellers, and no Greek was able to reach Syene and the lower cataracts during this reign. The trade through Ethiopia was wholly stopt, and the caravans went from Thebes to Cosseir to meet the ships which brought the goods of Arabia and India from the opposite coast of the Red Sea.

In the wars between Egypt and Asia Minor, in which Palestine had the misfortune to be the prize struggled for, and the debatable land on which the battles were fought, the Jews were often made to feel the difference between the stern pride of Antigonus and the milder temper of Ptolemy. The Egyptians of the Delta and the Jews had always been friends; and in the war which had ended with most of the Jewish nobles being led captive to Babylon, the Egyptians had helped them against the power of Nebuchadnezzar. Those who had at that time fled to Egypt, to avoid the cruelty of the conqueror, could hardly have felt themselves as strangers among the mixed race of Arabs, Phenicians, and Greeks, who formed so large a part of the trading population of the Delta. Hence, when Ptolemy treated the Jews with the same kindness that he did his own subjects, and held out the full privilege of Macedonian citizenship to those who would settle in his rising city of Alexandria, he was followed by crowds of industrious traders, manufacturers, and men of letters, who chose to live in Egypt in peace and wealth, rather than to stay in Palestine in the daily fear of having their houses sacked and burnt at every fresh quarrel between Ptolemy and Antigonus.

Josephus, Antiq. xii.

Among these Jews was the high-priest Hezekias, who was not more looked up to for his rank than for his eloquence and knowledge of mankind; and Mosollam, who was known for his bravery and skill as an archer. Hecatæus, who wrote a history of the Jews, gained his knowledge of the nation from the learned men who then followed Ptolemy into Egypt. He mentions Mosollam once riding out with a troop of soldiers, who, as they rode, were watching the flight of a bird that had been let loose by a soothsayer, to foretell what was going to happen; and Mosollam brought it down with an arrow from his bow, wittily remarking, that, as it could not foresee its own death, it certainly knew nothing about the fortunes of the soldiers.

Josephus, in Apionem.

No sooner was the peace agreed upon between the four generals, who were the most powerful kings in the known world, than Cassander, who held Macedonia, put to death Roxana, and her son the young Alexander Ægus, then thirteen years old, in whose name these generals had each governed his kingdom with unlimited sway, and who was then of an age that the soldiers, the givers of all power, were already planning to make him the real king of Macedonia, and of the wide conquests of his father.

Diod. Sic. lib. xix. B.C. 309.

The Macedonian phalanx, which formed the pride and sinews of every army, were equally held by their deep-rooted loyalty to the memory of Alexander, whether they were fighting for Ptolemy or for Antigonus, and equally thought that they were guarding a province for his heir; and it was through fear of loosening their hold upon the faithfulness of these their best troops, that Ptolemy and his rivals alike chose to govern their kingdoms under the unpretending title of lieutenants of the king of Macedonia. Hence, upon the death of Alexander Ægus, there was a throne, or at least a state prison, left empty for a new claimant.

Diod. Sic.
lib. xx.
Polysperchon, an old general of Alexander's army, then thought that he saw a way to turn Cassander out of Macedonia, by the help of Hercules, the natural son of Alexander by Barce; and having proclaimed him king, he led him with a strong army against Cassander. But Polysperchon wanted either courage or means for what he had undertaken, and he soon yielded to the bribes of Cassander, and put Hercules to death.

The children of Alexander having been in their turns murdered by their guardians, Cleopatra his sister was the only one left alive of the royal family of Macedonia. Almost every one of the generals had already courted a marriage with her, which had either been refused by herself or hindered by his rivals; and lastly Ptolemy, now that by the death of her nephews she brought kingdoms, or the love of the Macedonian mercenaries, which was worth more than kingdoms, as her dower, sent to ask her hand in marriage. This offer was accepted by Cleopatra, but on her journey from Sardis to Egypt, on her way to join her future husband, she was put to death by Antigonus. Thus every one who was of the family of Alexander paid the forfeit of life for that honour, and the death of Cleopatra ended the tragedy.

The treaty of peace between the generals seems never wholly to have stopped the warfare. Ptolemy was busy in helping the cities of Greece to gain their liberty, while Menelaus, his brother and admiral, was almost driven out of Cyprus by Demetrius. On this Ptolemy got together his fleet, to the number of one hundred and forty long gallies and two hundred transports, manned with not less than ten thousand men, and sailed with them to the help of his brother. This whole fleet under the command of Menelaus was met by Demetrius with the fleet of Antigonus, consisting of one hundred and twelve long gallies and a number of transports; and the Egyptian fleet, which had hitherto been master of the sea, was beaten near the city of Salamis in Cyprus by the smaller fleet of Demetrius. This was the heaviest loss that had ever befallen Ptolemy. Eighty long gallies were sunk, and forty long gallies with one hundred transports and eight thousand men were taken prisoners. He could no longer hope to keep Cyprus, and he sailed hastily back to Egypt, leaving to Demetrius the garrisons of the island as his prisoners, all of whom were enrolled in the army of Antigonus, to the number of sixteen thousand foot and six hundred horse.

This naval victory gave Demetrius the means of unburdening his proud mind of a debt of gratitude to his enemy; and accordingly, remembering what Ptolemy had done after the battle of Gaza, he sent back to Egypt, unasked for and unransomed, the whole of the prisoners who were of high rank, that is to say, the whole that had any choice about which side they fought for; and among them were Leontiscus the son, and Menelaus the brother, of Ptolemy.

Antigonus was overjoyed with the news of this victory, which, by lessening the power of Ptolemy, had done much to smooth his own path to the sovereignty of Alexander's empire, which was then

Plutarch.
Vit. Demet.

Justinus,
lib. xv. 2.

Diod. Sic.
lib. xx.
left without an heir; and he immediately took the title of king, and gave the same title to his son Demetrius. In this he was followed by Ptolemy and the other generals, but with this difference, that while Antigonus called himself king of all the provinces, Ptolemy called himself king of Egypt; and while Antigonus gained Syria and Cyprus, Ptolemy gained the friendship of every other kingdom, and of every free city in Greece: they all looked upon him as their best ally against Antigonus the common enemy.

B.C. 301.
The next year Antigonus mustered the whole of his forces in Cœlo-Syria, and got ready for a second attack upon Egypt. He had more than eighty thousand foot, eight thousand horse, and eighty-three elephants. Demetrius brought with him from Cyprus the fleet of one hundred and fifty long gallies, and one hundred transports laden with stores and engines of war. With this fleet, to which Ptolemy after his late loss had nothing that he could oppose, Antigonus had no need to ask leave of the Arabs of the little city of Petra, to march through their passes. But he led his army straight through the desert to Pelusium, while the ships of burden kept close to the shore with the stores. The pride of Antigonus would not let him follow the advice of the sailors, and wait eight days till the north winds of the spring equinox had passed; and by this haste many of his ships were wrecked on the coast, while others were driven into the Nile and fell into the hands of Ptolemy. Antigonus with the land forces found all the strong places well guarded by the Egyptian army; and being driven back at every point, discouraged by the loss of his ships, and by seeing whole bodies of his troops go over to Ptolemy, he at last took the advice of his officers and led back his army to Syria, while Ptolemy returned to Alexandria, to employ those powers of mind in the works of peace which he had so successfully used in war.

Antigonus then turned the whole weight of his mighty kingdom against the little island of Rhodes, which, though in sight of the coast of Asia Minor, held itself independent of him, and in close friendship with Ptolemy.

The island of Rhodes had from the earliest dawn of history held a high place among the states of Greece; and in all the arts of civilized life, in painting, sculpture, letters, and commerce, it had been lately rising in rank while the other free states had been falling. Its maritime laws were so highly thought of that they were copied by most other states, and being afterwards adopted into the Pandects of Justinian they have in part become the law of modern Europe; and it was the only state in which Greek liberty then kept its ground against the great empires of Alexander's successors.

Against this little state Demetrius led two hundred long gallies and one hundred and seventy transports, with more than forty thousand men. The whole of the Greek world looked on with the deepest interest while the veterans of Antigonus were again and again driven back from the walls of the blockaded city by its brave and virtuous citizens; who, while their houses were burning and their walls crumbling under the battering-ram, left the statues of Antigonus and Demetrius standing unhurt in the market-place, saved by their love of art and the remembrance of former kindness, which with a true greatness of mind they would not let the cruelties of the seige outweigh. The gallies of Ptolemy, though unable to keep at sea against the larger fleet of Demetrius, often forced their way into the harbour with the welcome supplies of corn. Month after month every stratagem and machine which the ingenuity of Demetrius could invent were tried and failed; and after the siege had lasted more than a year he was glad to find an excuse

Plutarch.
Vit. Demet.

Diod. Sic.
lib. xx.

for withdrawing his troops; and the Rhodians in their joy hailed Ptolemy with the title of Soter or *saviour*. This name he ever afterwards kept, though by the Greek writers he is more often called Ptolemy the son of Lagus, or Ptolemy Lagus.

If we search the history of the world for a second instance of so small an island daring to withstand the armies of so mighty an empire, we shall perhaps not find any one more remarkable than that of the same island. Seventeen hundred years afterwards it again drew upon itself the eyes of all the world, while it beat off the forces of the Ottoman empire under Mahomet II.; and, standing like a rock in front of the western world, it rolled back for years the tide of war, till its walls were at last crumbled to a heap of ruins by Solyman the Great, after a siege of many months.

One of the most valuable gifts which Egypt owed to Ptolemy was its coinage. Even Thebes " where treasures were largest in the houses," never was able to pass gold and silver from hand to hand without the trouble of weighing, and the doubt as to the fineness of the metal. The Greek merchants who crowded the markets of Canopus and Alexandria must have filled Lower Egypt with the coins of the cities from whence they came, all unlike one another in stamp and weight; but while every little city or even colony of Greece had its own coinage, Egypt had none. In the first years of his reign Ptolemy might well dislike coining; he would have been called upon to declare by the stamp upon the coin whether he was king of Egypt, and he seems not to have coined till after he had taken that title.

Visconti,
Icon. Grec.

His coins are of gold, silver, and copper, and are in a fine style of Greek workmanship. On the one side they bear the portrait of the king, without a beard, having the head bound with the royal diadem, which, unlike the modern crown of gold and precious stones, is a plain ribband tied in a bow behind. On the other side they have the words ΠΤΟΛΕΜΑΙΟΥ ΣΩΤΗΡΟΣ, ' *of Ptolemy Soter ;*' or ΒΑΣΙΛΕΩΣ ΠΤΟΛΕΜΑΙΟΥ, ' *of King Ptolemy,*' with an eagle standing upon a thunderbolt, which was only another way of drawing the eagle and sun, the hieroglyphical characters for the title Pharaoh. As the coins are not of the same weight as those of Greece, we must suppose that Ptolemy followed the Egyptian standard of weight; the drachma weighs fifty-five grains, making the talent of silver worth about one hundred and seventy pounds sterling. The cities in which the coins were struck in this reign seem to have been Abydus and Pelusium, if we are to judge by the letters on the coins; though we may be sure that they were also struck at Alexandria, but the coins of that city are not so marked.

The art of engraving coins did not flourish alone in Alexandria; painters and sculptors flocked to Egypt to enjoy the favours of Ptolemy. Apelles, indeed, whose paintings were thought by those Pliny,
lib. xxxv. 36. who had seen them to surpass any that had been before painted, or were likely to be painted, had quarrelled with Ptolemy, who had known him well when he was the friend and painter of Alexander. Once when he was at Alexandria, somebody wickedly told him that he was invited to dine at the royal table, and when Ptolemy angrily asked who it was that had sent his unwelcome guest, Apelles drew the face of the mischief-maker on the wall, and he was known to all the court by the likeness.

It was perhaps at one of these dinners, at which Ptolemy enjoyed Proclus,
Comm. ii. 4. the society of the men of letters, that he asked Euclid if he could not show him a shorter and easier way to the higher truths of mathematics than that by which he led the pupils in the Museum; and Euclid, as if to remind him of the royal roads of Persia, which ran by the side of the high-roads, but were kept clear and free for the king's own use, made him the well-known answer, that there was no royal road to geometry.

Diog. Laert. At another of these literary dinners, Diodorus Cronus the rhetorician, who is thought to have been the inventor of the Dilemma, was puzzled by a question put to him by Stilpo, and was so teazed by Ptolemy for not being able to answer it, that it was said to have embittered the rest of his life. This was the person against whom Callimachus some years later wrote a bitter epigram, beginning ' Cronus is a wise man.'

Pliny,
xxxv. 37. Antiphilus, who was born in Egypt and had studied painting under Ctesidemus, rose to high rank as a painter in Alexandria. Among his best-known pictures were the bearded Bacchus, the xxxv. 40. young Alexander, and Hippolitus afraid of a bull. His boy, blowing up a fire with his mouth, was much praised for the mouth of the boy, and for the light and shade of the room. His Ptolemy Lucian.
de Calumniâ. hunting was also highly thought of. He showed a mean jealousy of Apelles, and accused him of joining in a plot against the king, for which Apelles narrowly escaped punishment; but when Ptolemy found that the charge was untrue he sent him a gift of one hundred talents to make amends.

The angry feelings of Apelles were by no means cooled by this gift, but they boiled over in his great picture of Calumny. On the right of the picture sat Ptolemy, holding out his hand to Calumny who was coming up to him. On each side of the king stood a woman who seemed meant for Ignorance and Suspicion. Calumny was a beautiful maiden, but with anger and deep-rooted malice in her face; in her left hand was a lighted torch, and with her right she was dragging along by the hair a young man, who was stretching forth his hands to heaven and calling upon the gods to bear witness that he was guiltless. Before her walked Envy, a pale, hollow-eyed, diseased man, perhaps a portrait of the accuser; and behind were two women, Craft and Deceit, who were encouraging and supporting her. At a distance stood Repentance, in the ragged black garb of mourning, who was turning away her face for shame as Truth came up to her.

Ptolemy Soter was plain in his manners, and scarcely passed his own generals in the costliness of his way of life. He often supped and slept at the houses of his friends; and his own house had so little of the palace that he borrowed dishes and tables of his friends when he asked any number of them to sup with him in return, saying that it was the part of a king to enrich others rather than to be rich himself.

Plutarch.
Apophthegm.

Before he took the title of king he was styled by friendly states by the simple name of Ptolemy the Macedonian; and during the whole of his reign he was as far from being overbearing or tyrannical in his behaviour as from being kinglike in his dress and household. Once when he wished to laugh at a boasting antiquarian, he asked him, what he knew could not be answered, who was the father of Peleus; and the other let his wit so far get the better of his prudence as in return to ask the king, who had never heard the name of his grandfather, if he knew who was the father of Lagus. But Ptolemy took no further notice of this than to remark that if a king cannot bear rude answers he ought not to ask rude questions.

Pausanias,
lib. vi. 3; x. 7.

Plutarch.
de Irâ cohib.

An answer which Ptolemy once made to a soothsayer might almost be taken as the proverb which had guided him through life. When his soldiers met with an anchor in one of their marches, and were discouraged by being told by the soothsayer that it was a proof that they ought to stop where they then were, the king answered, that an anchor was an omen of safety, not of delay.

Appian.
Syriac. 56.

Athenæus,
lib. xiii. 5.
Justinus,
lib. xv. 2.
Ptolemy first married Thais the noted courtesan, but their sons seem not to have been thought legitimate. Leontiscus, the eldest, we afterwards hear of, fighting bravely against Demetrius; of the second, named Lagus after his grandfather, we hear nothing.

Pausanias,
lib. i. 6.
lib. i. 16.
He then married Eurydice the daughter of Antipater, by whom he had several children. The eldest son, Ptolemy, was named Ceraunus, *the Thunderer,* and was banished by his father from Alexandria. In his distress he fled to Seleucus, by whom he was kindly received; but after the death of Ptolemy Soter he basely Memnon,
ap. Photium. plotted against Seleucus and put him to death. He then defeated in battle Antigonus the son of Demetrius, and got possession of Macedonia for a short time. He married his half-sister Arsinoë, and put her children to death; and was soon afterwards put to death himself by the Gauls, who were either fighting against him or were mercenaries in his own army. His Macedonian coins, with Goltzius,
iii. 37. the name Ptolemy Ceraunus, prove that he took the name himself, and that it was not a nickname given to him for his ungovernable temper, as has been sometimes thought.

Pausanias,
lib. i. 7.
Another son of Ptolemy and Eurydice was put to death by Ptolemy Philadelphus, for plotting against his throne, to which, as the elder brother, he might have thought himself the best entitled.

lib. i. 9, 10.
Their daughter Lysandra married Agathocles the son of Lysimachus; but when Agathocles was put to death by his father, she fled to Egypt with her children, and put herself under the care of Ptolemy.

lib. i. 6.
Ptolemy's second wife was Berenice, a lady who came into Egypt with Eurydice, and formed part of her household. She was the widow of a man named Philip, and had by her first husband one son, named Magas, whom Ptolemy made governor of Cyrene.

Perhaps all young queens may be beautiful in the eyes of the poet; but the following lines, by Asclepiades of Samos, on mistaking the picture of Berenice for that of Venus, may be quoted for their neatness, if not to prove the queen's beauty.

> ' This form is Cytherea's;—nay
> 'Tis Berenice's, I protest:
> So like to both, you safely may
> Give it to either you like best.'

Anthol. Græc. Merivale.

With Berenice, Ptolemy spent the rest of his life without any thing to trouble the happiness of his family. He saw their elder son Ptolemy, whom we must call by the name which he took late in life—Philadelphus, grow up every thing that he could wish him to be; and, moved alike by his love for the mother and by the good qualities of the son, he chose him as his successor on the throne, instead of his eldest son Ptolemy Ceraunus, who had shown, by every act in his life, his unfitness for the trust.

His daughter Arsinoë married Lysimachus in his old age, and urged him against his son Agathocles, the husband of her own sister. She afterwards married her half-brother Ptolemy Ceraunus; and lastly, we shall see her the wife of her brother Philadelphus.

Pausanias, lib. i. 10.

Justinus, lib. xvii. 2.

Argæus, his youngest son, was put to death by Philadelphus, on a charge of treason.

Pausanias, lib. i. 7.

Of his youngest daughter Philotera we know nothing, except that her brother Philadelphus afterwards named a city of Ethiopia after her.

Strabo, lib. xv.

In the last defeat of Demetrius, Ptolemy had regained Cœlo-Syria and Cyprus; and his throne became stronger as his life drew to an end. With a wisdom rare in kings and conquerors, he had never let his ambition pass his means; he never aimed at universal power; and he was led, both by his kind feelings and wise policy, to befriend all those states which like his own were threatened by that mad ambition in others.

Justinus, lib. xvi. 2. His last public act, in the thirty-eighth year of his reign, was ordered by the same wisdom and forbearance which had governed every part of his life. Feeling the weight of years press heavily upon him—that he was less able than formerly to bear the duties of his office, and wishing to see his son firmly seated on the throne, he laid aside his diadem and his title, proclaimed Ptolemy, his son by Berenice, king, and contented himself with the modest rank of somatophylax, or satrap, to his successor.

This is perhaps the most successful instance known of a king, who had been used to be obeyed by armies and by nations, willingly giving up his power when he found his bodily strength no longer equal to it. Charles V. gave up the empire in disappointment, and hid himself in a monastery to avoid the sight of any thing which could remind him of his former greatness. Diocletian, who, more like a philosopher, did not refuse to hear news from the world of politics which he had left, had his last days embittered and his life shortened by witnessing the misconduct of his successors. But Ptolemy Soter had the happiness of having a son willing to follow in the track which he had laid down for him, and of living to see the wisdom of his own laws proved by the well-being of the kingdom under his successor.

But while we are watching the success of Ptolemy's plans, and the rise of this Greek monarchy at Alexandria, we cannot help being pained with the thought that the Copts of Upper Egypt are forgotten, and asking whether it would not have been still better to have raised Thebes to the place which it once held, and to have recalled the days of Rameses, instead of trying, what might seem the hopeless task, to plant Greek arts in Africa.

But a review of this history will show that, as far as human fore-thought can judge, this could not have been done. If Thebes had only fallen on the conquest by Cambyses—if the rebellions against the Persians had been those of Copts throwing off their chains and struggling for freedom,—we might have hoped to have seen Egypt, on the fall of Darius, again rise under kings of the blood and language of the people; and we should have thought the gilded and half-hid chains of the Ptolemies were little better than the heavy yoke of the Persians.

This, however, is very far from having been the case. We first see the kings of Lower Egypt guarding their thrones at Sais by Greek soldiers; and then, that every struggle of Inarus, of Necta-nebo, and of Tachus, against the Persians, was only made by the courage and arms of Greeks hired in the Delta by Egyptian gold. During the three hundred years before Alexander was hailed by Egypt as its deliverer, scarcely once had the Copts, trusting to their own courage, stood up in arms against either Persians or Greeks; and the country was only then conquered without a battle, because the power and arms were already in the hands of the Greeks; because in the mixt races of the Delta the Greeks were so far the strongest, though not the most numerous, that a Greek kingdom rose there with the same ease, and for the same reasons, that an Arab kingdom rose in the same place nine centuries later.

National character, national pride, love of country, and the better feelings of clanship, are the chief grounds upon which a great people can be raised. These feelings are closely allied to self-denial, or a willingness on the part of each man to give up much for the good of the whole. By this, chiefly, public monuments are built, and citizens stand by one another in battle; and these feel-ings were certainly strong in Upper Egypt in the days of its greatness. But, when the throne was moved to Lower Egypt—when the kingdom was governed by the kings of Sais, and even afterwards, when it was struggling against the Persians,—these virtues were wanting: few public buildings were raised, though the country was overflowing with wealth, and they trusted to foreign hirelings in their struggle for freedom. The Delta was peopled by three races of men—Copts, Greeks, and Phenicians or Arabs; and even before the sceptre was given to the Greeks by Alexander's conquests it would seem as if the Copts had lost the power to hold it.

PTOLEMY PHILADELPHUS.

FEW princes ever mounted a throne with such fair prospects B.C. 284. before them as the second Ptolemy. He had been brought up with great care, and being a younger son was not spoilt by that flattery which in all courts is so freely offered to the heir. He was born in the island of Cos; his first tutor in letters and philosophy was Suidas. Philetas, of Cos, an author of some elegies and epigrams now lost; and as he grew up he found himself surrounded by the phi_ losophers and writers with whom his father mixed on the easiest terms of friendship. During the long reign of Ptolemy Soter the people had been made happy by wise and good laws, trade had flourished, the cities had grown rich, and the fortresses had been strengthened. The troops were well trained, their loyalty un- doubted, and the Egyptians, instead of being distrusted as slaves, were armed and disciplined like the Macedonians. The population Diod. Sic.
lib. i. 31. of the country was counted at seven millions. Alexandria, the capital of the kingdom, was not only the largest trading city in the world, but was one of the most favoured seats of learning. It surely must have been easy to foresee that the prince then mounting the throne, even if but slightly gifted with virtues, would give his name to a reign which could not be otherwise than remarkable in the history of Egypt. But Philadelphus, though, like his father, he was not free from the vices of his times and of his rank, had more of wisdom than is usually the lot of kings; and though we cannot but see that he was only watering the plants and gathering the fruit where his father had planted, and that like Lorenzo de’ Medici he has received the praise for reaping the harvest which is due to the father for his wisdom in sowing the seed, yet we must at the same time acknowledge that Philadelphus was a successor worthy of Ptolemy Soter.

The first act of his reign, or rather the last of his father’s reign, was the proclamation, or the ceremony of showing the new king to the troops and people. All that was dazzling, all that was costly or curious, all that the wealth of Egypt could buy or the gratitude of the provinces could give, was brought forth to grace this religious show, which was copied rather from the triumphs of Rameses and Thothmosis, than from anything that had been seen in Greece.

Athenæus, lib. v.
The procession began with the pomp of Osiris, at the head of which were the Sileni in scarlet and purple cloaks, who opened the way through the crowd. Twenty satyrs followed, on each side of the road, bearing torches; and then Victories with golden wings, clothed in skins, each with a golden staff six cubits long, twined round with ivy. An altar was carried next, covered with golden ivy-leaves, with a garland of golden vine-leaves tied with white ribands; and this was followed by a hundred and twenty boys, in scarlet frocks, carrying bowls of crocus, myrrh, and frankincense. Then came forty satyrs crowned with golden ivy-leaves, with their naked bodies stained with gay colours, each carrying a crown of vine-leaves and gold. Then two Sileni in scarlet cloaks and white boots, one having the hat and wand of Mercury and the other a trumpet; and between them walked a man, six feet high, in tragic dress and mask, meant for the Year, carrying a golden cornucopia. He was followed by a tall and beautiful woman, meant for the Lustrum of five years, carrying in one hand a crown and in the other a palm-branch. Then came an altar and a troop of satyrs,

in gold and scarlet, carrying golden wine-vases and drinking-cups.

Then came Philiscus the poet, the priest of Osiris, with all the servants of the god. Then the Delphic tripods, the prizes which were to be given in the wrestling matches; that for the boys was nine cubits high, and that for the men twelve cubits high. Next came a four-wheeled car, fourteen cubits long and eight wide, drawn along by one hundred and eighty men, on which was the statue of Osiris, fifteen feet high, pouring wine out of a golden vase, and having a scarlet frock down to his feet, with a yellow transparent robe over it, and over all a scarlet cloak. Before the statue was a large golden bowl, and a tripod with bowls of incense on it. Over the whole was an awning of ivy and vine-leaves; and in the same chariot were the priests and priestesses of the god.

This was followed by a smaller chariot drawn by sixty men, in which was the statue of Isis in a robe of yellow and gold. Then came a chariot full of grapes, and another with a large cask of wine, which was poured out on the road as the procession moved on; and then another band of satyrs and Sileni, and more chariots of wine. Then eighty Delphic vases of silver, and Panathenaic and other vases; and sixteen hundred dancing boys in white frocks and golden crowns. Then a number of beautiful pictures; and a chariot carrying a grove of trees, out of which flew pigeons and doves, so tied that they might be easily caught by the crowd.

On another chariot drawn by an elephant came Osiris, as he returned from his Indian conquests. He was followed by twenty-four chariots drawn by elephants, sixty drawn by goats, twelve by lions, seven by rhinoceroses, four by wild asses, fifteen by buffaloes, eight by ostriches, and seven by stags. Then came chariots loaded with the tributes of the conquered nations; men of Ethiopia car-

Athenæus,
lib. v.
rying six hundred elephants' teeth; sixty huntsmen leading two thousand four hundred dogs; and one hundred and fifty men carrying trees, in the branches of which were tied parrots and other beautiful birds. Next walked the foreign animals, Ethiopian and Arabian sheep, Brahmin bulls, a white bear, leopards, panthers, bears, a camelopard, and a rhinoceros.

In another chariot was seen Bacchus running away from Juno, and flying to the altar of Rhea. After that came the statues of Alexander and Ptolemy Soter crowned with gold and ivy: by the side of Ptolemy stood the statues of Virtue, of the god Chem, and of the city of Corinth; and he was followed by female statues of the conquered cities of Ionia, Greece, Asia Minor, and Persia; and the statues of the other gods. Then came crowds of singers and cymbal-players, and two thousand bulls with gilt horns, crowns, and breast-plates.

Then came Amun-Ra and the other gods; and the statue of Alexander between Victory and the goddess Neith, in a chariot drawn by elephants: then a number of thrones of ivory and gold; and on one was a golden crown, on another a golden cornucopia, and on the throne of Ptolemy Soter was a crown worth ten thousand *aurei*, or nearly six thousand pounds sterling: then three thousand two hundred golden crowns, twenty golden shields, sixty-four suits of golden armour; and the whole was closed with forty waggons of silver vessels, twenty of golden vessels, eighty of scents, and fifty-seven thousand six hundred foot soldiers, and twenty-three thousand two hundred horse. The procession began moving by torch-light before the sun rose in the morning, and the sun set in the evening before it had all passed.

It went through the streets of Alexandria to the royal tents on the outside of the city, where, as in the procession, every thing that was costly in art, or scarce in nature, was brought together in honour of the day. At the public games, Ptolemy Soter was presented with twenty golden crowns, Berenice with twenty-three, and their son the new king with twenty, beside other costly gifts; and two thousand two hundred and thirty-nine talents, or four hundred thousand pounds, were spent on the amusements of the day. For the account of this curious procession we are indebted to Callixenes of Rhodes, who was then travelling in Egypt, and who wrote a history of Alexandria.

One of the earliest troubles in the reign of Philadelphus was the revolt of Cyrene. The government of that part of Africa had been entrusted to Magas, the half-brother of the king, son of Berenice by her former husband. Berenice, who had been successful in setting aside Ceraunus to make room for her son Philadelphus on the throne of Egypt, has even been said to have favoured the rebellious and ungrateful efforts of her elder son Magas to make himself king of Cyrene.

Pausanias, lib. i. 7.

Magas, without waiting till the large armies of Egypt were drawn together to crush his little state, marched hastily towards Alexandria, in the hopes of being joined by some of the restless thousands of that crowded city. But he was quickly recalled to Cyrene by the news of the rising of the Marmaridæ, the race of Libyan herdsmen who had been driven back from the coast by the Greek settlers who founded Cyrene. Philadelphus then led his army along the coast against the rebels; but he was, in the same way, stopt by the fear of treachery among his own Gallic mercenaries.

More than a century before this time, the Celts, or Gauls, had found their own forests too crowded for their way of life, and, moving southward, had overrun the fair plains of the north of Italy, and nearly crushed imperial Rome in the cradle. Other bands of these fierce barbarians had wandered as far as Greece, where their wild and unarmed courage could do little against the spears of the Macedonian phalanx. But the large armies which were called out by the quarrels of Alexander's successors could not be raised without the help of barbarians, and in these ranks the Gauls found the pay and plunder for which they had left their own forests. Thus, we meet with them in the armies of Egypt, of Macedonia, and of Asia Minor; and in this last country they afterwards settled, and gave their own name to the province of Galatia.

Philadelphus had reason to believe that four thousand of these Gauls, who formed part of the army which he was leading against Cyrene, were secretly plotting against him. Therefore, with a measured cruelty which the use of foreign mercenaries could alone have taught him, he led back his army to the marshes of the Delta, and, entrapping the four thousand distrusted Gauls in one of the small islands, he hemmed them in between the water and the spears of the phalanx, and they all died miserably, by famine, by drowning, or by the sword.

Magas had married Apime, the daughter of Antiochus Soter, king of Syria; and he sent to his father-in-law to beg him to march upon Cœlo-Syria and Palestine, to call off the army of Philadelphus from Cyrene. But Philadelphus did not wait for this attack: his armies moved before Antiochus was ready, and, by a successful inroad upon Syria, he prevented any relief being sent to Magas.

Pausanias,
lib. i. 6.
Justinus,
lib. xxvi. 3.
After the war between the brothers had lasted five years, Magas made an offer of peace, which was to be sealed by a marriage between his only child Berenice and the son of Philadelphus. To this offer Philadelphus yielded; as by the death of Magas, who was already worn out by luxury and disease, Cyrene would then fall to his own son. Magas, indeed, died before the marriage took place;

but, notwithstanding the efforts made by his widow to break the agreement, the treaty was kept, and on this marriage Cyrene again formed part of the kingdom of Egypt.

But the black spot upon the character of Philadelphus, which all the blaze of science and letters by which he was surrounded cannot make us overlook, is the death of two of his brothers. A son of Eurydice, who might perhaps have thought that he was robbed of the throne of Egypt by his younger brother, and who was unsuccessful in raising the island of Cyprus in rebellion; and a younger brother, Argæus, who was also charged with joining in a plot, both lost their lives by his orders. Well might the historians believe that the name of Philadelphus, which he took to show his love for a sister, was given him as a reproach for the murder of two brothers and the war of five years against a third.

Pausanias, lib. i. 7.

In reviewing the history of the world during past ages, we place ourselves, in thought, at each century, on that spot of the earth on which the historians of the time lived; and from that spot, as from a height, we look over the other kingdoms of the world as far countries, about which we know nothing but what is known at the place where we then stand. Thus, in the time of Moses, we live in Egypt and in the desert; in the reign of Solomon at Jerusalem; in the time of Pericles at Athens; and in the reigns of Ptolemy Soter and Philadelphus at Alexandria. But knowing, as we must know, of the after greatness of Rome, and that in a few ages we shall have to stand on the capitol, and hear news from the distant province of Egypt, it is with peculiar interest that we hear for the first time that the bravery and rising power of the Romans had forced themselves into the notice of Philadelphus. Pyrrhus, the king of Macedon, had been beaten by the Romans, and driven out of Italy; and the king of Egypt thought it not beneath him to send

Livy, xiv. 38. B.C. 274.

an ambassador to the senate, to wish them joy of their success, and to make a treaty of peace with the republic. The embassy, as we might suppose, was received in Rome with great joy; and four ambassadors—three of the proud name of Fabius, with Quintus Ogulnius—were sent back to seal the treaty.

Philadelphus gave them some costly gifts, probably those usually given to ambassadors; but Rome was then young, her citizens had not yet made gold the end for which they lived, and the ambassadors returned the gifts, for they could receive nothing beyond the
thanks of the senate for having done their duty. This treaty was never broken; and when, soon afterwards, the Carthaginians, in their war with Rome, sent to Alexandria to beg for a loan of two thousand talents, Philadelphus refused it, saying that he would help them against his enemies, but not against his friends.

From that time forward we find Egypt in alliance with Rome; but we also find that they were day by day changing place with one another: Egypt soon began to sink, while Rome was rising in power; Egypt soon received help from her stronger ally, and at last became a province of the Roman empire.

At the time of this embassy, when Greek arts were nearly unknown to the Romans, the ambassadors must have seen much that was new to them, and much that was worth copying; and three years afterwards, when two of them, Quintus Ogulnius and Caius Fabius Pictor, were chosen consuls, they coined silver for the first time in Rome. With them begins the series of consular denarii, which throws such light on Roman history.

About the middle of this reign, Berenice, the mother of the king, died; and it was most likely then that Philadelphus began to date from the beginning of his own reign: he had before gone on dating like his father, from the beginning of his father's reign.

In the year after her death, the feast of Osiris, in the month of Mesore, was celebrated at Alexandria with more than usual pomp by the queen Arsinoë. Venus, or Isis, had just raised Berenice to heaven, and Arsinoë, in return, showed her gratitude by the sums of money spent on the feast of Osiris, or Adonis as he was sometimes called by the Greeks. Theocritus, who was there, wrote a poem on the day, and tells us of the crowds in the streets, of the queen's gifts to the temple, and of the beautiful tapestries, on which were woven the figures of the god and goddess, breathing as if alive.

Among other buildings, Philadelphus raised a temple in honour of his father and mother, and placed in it their statues, made of ivory and gold, and ordered that they should be worshipped like the gods and other kings of the country.

In this reign was finished the light-house on the island of Pharos, as a guide to ships when entering the harbour of Alexandria by night. It was built by the architect Sostratus, and as it had been planned and begun by the orders of Ptolemy Soter, it was dedicated 'to the gods Soteres,' as Soter and Berenice were called in all public writings. The building of the royal burial-place in Alexandria, which had been begun by Ptolemy Soter, was also finished, and Philadelphus removed the body of Alexander to it from Memphis, where it had for the time been left.

The navigation of the Red Sea, along which the wind blows hard from the north for nine months in the year, was found so dangerous by the coasting vessels from the south of Arabia, that they always chose the most southerly port in which they could meet the Egyptian buyers. Hence, when Philadelphus had made the whole of Upper Egypt to the cataracts as quiet and safe for merchants as the Delta, he made a new port on the Red Sea nearly two hundred miles to the south of Cosseir, and named it Berenice, after his mother.

Theocritus, Idyll. 15.

Idyll. 17.

Strabo, lib. xvii.

Pausanias, lib. i. 7.

Diod. Sic. lib. i.

Pliny, lib. vi. 26.

He also built four public inns or watering houses, where the caravans might find water for the camels on their twelve days' journey through the desert from Coptos to this new port.

Wilkinson's Thebes.
The temple of Isis at Philæ, an island in the Nile near Syene, was begun in this reign, though not finished till some reigns later. It is still the wonder of travellers, and by its size and style proves the wealth and good taste of the priests.

Pliny, lib. vi. 33.
Philadelphus also built a city at the head of the Red Sea, where Suez now stands, and named it Arsinoë, after his sister; and he finished the canal which Sesostris and Darius had begun, by which ships could pass from this city on the Red Sea to the Nile near
lib. vi. 34.
Pelusium. He also built a second city of the name of Berenice, called the Troglodytic Berenice, on the coast of the Red Sea, in the same latitude as Meroë the capital of Ethiopia, and most likely on the site of the port to which the Ethiopian traders had gone to meet the vessels from Arabia, in those years when the trade came to Egypt through Ethiopia.

In the number of ports which were then growing into the rank of cities, we see full proof of the great trade of Egypt at that time: and we may form some opinion of the profit which was gained from
lib. vi. 36.
the trade of the Red Sea, from the report of Clitarchus to Alexander, that the people of one of the islands would give a talent of gold for a horse; so plentiful with them was gold, and so scarce the useful animals of Europe.

lib. vi. 34.
In the same latitude with the Troglodytic Berenice, but separated from it by one of the forests of Ethiopia, was the new city of Ptolemais, which, however, was little more than a post from which the hunting parties went out to catch elephants for the armies of
Hieronymus, in Dan. xi.
Egypt. Asia had been the only country from which the armies had been supplied with elephants before Philadelphus brought them

from Ethiopia. It was most likely about the same time that the Carthaginians began to use elephants in their armies, as, on a coin struck by Atilius Calatinus, the Roman proconsul, on his conquering the Carthaginians in Sicily, in the twenty-ninth year of this reign, the triumphal car is drawn by four elephants. Goltzius de Re Numm. Livy, lib. xvii. 29.

The Museum of Alexandria held at this time the highest rank among the Greek schools, whether for poetry, mathematics, astronomy, or medicine, the four branches into which it was divided. Its library held two hundred thousand rolls of papyrus; which, however, could hardly have been equal to ten thousand printed volumes. Many of these were bought by Philadelphus in Athens and Rhodes; and his copy of Aristotle's works was bought of the philosopher Nileus, a noted book-collector. Josephus, Antiq. xii. 2.

Athenæus, lib. i. 2.

At the head of this library had been Demetrius Phalereus, who, after ruling Athens with great praise, was banished from his country, and fled to Ptolemy Soter. He was at the same time the most learned and the most polished of orators. 'He brought learning from the closet into the forum, and, by the soft turn which he gave to public speaking, made that sweet and lovely which had before been grave and solemn.' Cicero thought him the great master in the art of speaking, and seems to have taken him as the model upon which he wished to form his own style. He wrote upon philosophy, history, government, and poetry; but the only one of his works which has reached to our time is his treatise on elocution; and the careful thought which he there gives to the choice of words, and to the form of a sentence, and even the parts of a sentence, show the value then set upon style. He not only advised Ptolemy Soter what books he should buy, but which he should read, and he chiefly recommended those on government and policy; and it is alike to the credit of the king and of the librarian Hieronymus, in Dan. xi.

Cicero, Brut.

Suidas.

Plutarch. Regum apophthegm.

that he put before him books which, from their praise of freedom and hatred of tyrants, few persons would even speak of in the presence of a king.

Diog. L aert. But Demetrius had also been consulted by Soter about the choice of a successor, and had given his opinion that the crown ought to be left to his eldest son, and that wars would arise between his children if it were not so left; hence we can hardly wonder that, on the death of Soter, Demetrius should have been ordered to leave Alexandria.

Suidas. Soon after this, we find Zenodotus of Ephesus filling the office of librarian to the Museum. He was a poet, who, with others, had been employed by Soter in the education of his children. He was also a critic, and is known as the first who turned his thoughts towards mending the text of Homer, which had become faulty through the carelessness of the copiers.

At the head of the mathematical school was Euclid, who is, however, less known to us by what his pupils have said of him than by his own work, which is one of the few of the scientific writings of the ancients which have come down to us. The discoveries of the man of science are made use of by his successor, and the discoverer perhaps loses part of his reward when his writings are passed by, after they have served us as a stepping-stone to mount by. If he wishes his works to live with those of the poet and orator, he must, like them, cultivate those beauties of style which are fitted to his matter. Euclid did so: and the Elements have been for more than two thousand years the model for all writers on geometry. He begins at the beginning, and leads the learner, step by step, from the simplest propositions, called axioms, which rest upon metaphysical rather than mathematical proof, to high geometrical truths. The mind is, indeed, sometimes wearied by being made to stop at every single step in the path, and wishes with Ptolemy Soter for a shorter road; but, upon the whole, Euclid's neatness and clearness have never been equalled. The writings of Hippocrates, Eudoxus, Proclus, Comm. ii. 4. Leon, Theatetus, and others, from which the Elements were compiled, are now lost, and their names hardly known; while the writings of Euclid will, from their style and manner, be read as long as geometry is studied.

Ctesibius ranked equally high in mixed mathematics, although Athenæus, lib. ix. Pliny, lib. vii. 38. his name is now little known; he wrote on the theory of hydrostatics, and was the inventor of several water-engines; an application of mathematics which was much called for by the artificial irrigation of Egypt.

Among the best known of the men of letters who now came to Alexandria to enjoy the patronage of Philadelphus was Theocritus. He was born or at least brought up at Syracuse. Many of his poems are now lost, but his pastoral poems and elegies, though too rough for the polished taste of Quinctillian, and perhaps more like nature than we wish any works of imitative art to be, have always been looked upon as the model of that kind of poetry. He repaid the bounty of the king in the way most agreeable to him; he boasted that he would in an undying poem place him in the rank of the demi-gods; and assured him, with the Pyramids and the Memnonium before his eyes, that generosity toward the poets would do more to make his name live for ever than any building that he could raise.

The muse of Theocritus is wholly Sicilian; he has drawn no pictures from the country to which he had removed. He hardly mentions Egypt; when he writes to please himself, his thoughts wander over Sicily; when he writes through gratitude, they are imprisoned in the court of Alexandria.

Suidas. In a narrow back street of Alexandria lived the poet Callimachus, earning his livelihood by teaching. But the writer of the hymns could not long dwell so near the court of Philadelphus unknown and unhonoured. He was made professor of poetry in the Museum, and even now repays the king and patron for what he then received. He was a man of great industry, and wrote in prose and in all kinds of verse; but of these only a few hymns and epigrams have come down to our time. He was born at Cyrene, and though, from the language in which he wrote, his thoughts are mostly Greek, yet he did not forget the place of his birth.

Hymn to Apollo.
Hymn to Delos. He calls upon Apollo by the name of Carneus, because, after Sparta and Thera, Cyrene was his chosen seat. He paints Latona, weary and in pain in the island of Delos, as leaning against a palm-tree, by the side of the river Inopus, which sinking into the ground was to rise again in Egypt near the cataracts of Syene: and prettily pointing to Philadelphus, he makes Apollo, yet unborn, ask his mother not to give birth to him in the island of Cos, because that island was already chosen as the birth-place of another god, the child of the gods Soteres, who would be the copy of his father, and under whose diadem both Egypt and the islands would be proud to be governed by a Macedonian.

Cicero, Brut. Hegesias of Cyrene was an early lecturer on philosophy at Alexandria. His short and broken sentences were laughed at by Cicero, Tusc. Quæst. i. 34. yet he was so much listened to, when lecturing against the fear of death, and showing that in quitting life we leave behind us more pains than pleasures, that he was stopt by Ptolemy Soter through fear of his causing self-murder among his hearers. He then wrote a book upon the same subject, for though the state watched over the public teaching, it took no notice of books; so little power had authors of spreading their opinions.

Philostephanus of Cyrene, the friend of Callimachus, was a naturalist who wrote upon fishes, and is the first we hear of who limited his studies to one branch of natural history. Athenæus, lib. viii.

But Cyrene did not send all its great men to Alexandria; it had a school of its own, which gave its name to the Cyrenaic sect. The founder of this sect was Aristippus, the pupil of Socrates, who had the high honour of being present at his death. He was the first philosopher who took money from his pupils, and used to say that they valued their lessons more for having to pay for them; but he was much blamed by his brethren for thus lowering the dignity of the teacher. He died several years before Ptolemy Soter came into Egypt. Strabo, lib. xvii. Diog. Laert.

The Cyrenaic sect thought happiness, not goodness, was the end to be aimed at through life, and selfishness, rather than kindness to others, the right spring of men's actions. It would hardly be fair to take their opinions from the mouths of their enemies; and the dialogues of Socrates with their founder, as told to us by Xenophon, would prove a lower tone of morality than he is likely to have held. But often as this false rule has been set up for our guidance, there have always been found many to make use of it in a way not meant by the teacher. The Cyrenaic sect soon fell into the disrepute to which these principles were likely to lead it, and wholly ceased when Epicurus taught the same opinions more philosophically. Memorabilia.

The chair of philosophy at Cyrene was afterwards filled by Arete the daughter of Aristippus; and after her death by her son Aristippus, who, having been brought up in the lecture-room of his mother, was called, in order to distinguish him from his grandfather of the same name, Metrodidactus, or *mother-taught*. History has not told us whether he took this name himself in gratitude for the debt which he owed this learned lady, or whether it was given him by his pupils; but in either case it was a sure way of giving to the mother the fame which was due to her for the education of her son; for no one can fail to ask what was the name of the mother of Metrodidactus.

Diog. Laert. Theodorus, one of the pupils of Metrodidactus, though at one time banished from Cyrene, rose to high honour under Philadelphus, and was sent by him as ambassador to Lysimachus.

Strato, the pupil of Theophrastus, though chiefly known for his writings on physics, was also a writer on many branches of knowledge. He was one of the men of learning who had taken part in the education of Philadelphus; and the king showed his gratitude to his teacher, by making him a present of eighty talents or thirteen thousand pounds sterling. He was for eighteen years at the head of one of the schools of Alexandria.

Ptolemy, Syntax. Mag. lib. vii. 3. Timocharis the astronomer began his observations at Alexandria in the last reign, and continued them through half of this reign. He began a catalogue of the fixed stars, with their latitudes and their longitudes measured from the equinoctial point; by the help of which Hipparchus, one hundred and fifty years afterwards, found that the equinoctial point had moved. He has left an observation of the place of Venus, on the seventeenth day of the month of Dr. Young, Astron. Col. Mesore, in the thirteenth year of this reign, which by the modern tables of the planets is known to have been on the eighth day of October, B.C. 272; from which we learn that the first year of Philadelphus ended in October, B.C. 284, and the first year of Ptolemy Soter ended in October, B.C. 322.

Ptolemy, Syntax. Mag. lib. vii. 3. Aristillus also made observations of the same kind at Alexandria. Few of them have been handed down to us, but they were made use of by Hipparchus.

Aristarchus the astronomer of Samos most likely came to Alex- Ptolemy, Syntax. Mag. lib. iii. 2. andria in the last reign, as some of his observations were made in the very beginning of the reign of Philadelphus. He is the first astronomer who is known to have taken the true view of the solar system. He said that the sun was the centre round which the Archimedes, apud Wallis. earth moved in a circle; and, as if he had foreseen that even in after ages we should not be able to measure the distance of the fixed stars, he said that the earth's yearly path bore no greater proportion to the concave heavens in which the stars were set than the point without size in the centre of a circle does to its circumference. But the work in which he proved these great truths, or perhaps threw out these happy guesses, is lost; and the astronomers who followed him clung to the old belief that the earth was the centre round which the sun moved. The only writings of Aristarchus which now remain are his short work on the distances and magnitudes of the sun and moon.

Aratus, who was born in Cyprus, is sometimes counted among Suidas. Tzetzes, in Lycophronte. the pleiades or seven stars of Alexandria. His Phænomena is a short astronomical poem, which scarcely aims at any of the grace or flow of poetry. It describes the planets and the constellations one by one, and tells us what stars are seen in the head, feet, and other parts of each figure; and then the seasons, and the stars seen at night, at each time of the year. At a time when maps were little known, it must have been found of the greatest use, in giving to learners, who wished to know the names of the stars, that knowledge which we now gain from globes; and its being in verse made it the more easy to remember. The value which the ancients set upon this poem is curiously shown by the number of Latin translations which were made from it.

Cicero in his early youth, before he was known as an orator or philosopher, perhaps before he himself knew in which of the paths of letters he was soon to take the lead, translated this poem ; and it is not a little proof of the high place which Cicero's writings held in the opinions of those with whom he lived, that this is perhaps the only copy of school-boys' verses which has come down to us from the ancients.

The next translation is by Germanicus Cæsar, whose early death and many good qualities have thrown such a bright light upon his name. He shone as a general, as an orator, and as an author ; but his Greek comedies, his Latin orations, and his poem on Augustus, are all lost, while his translation of Aratus is all that is left, to prove that this high name in literature was not given to him for his political virtues alone.

Lastly Avienus, a writer in the reign of Diocletian, or perhaps of Theodosius, has left a rugged unpolished translation of this much valued poem.

Athenæus,
lib. xi. 12. Sosibius was one of the rhetoricians of the Museum who lived upon the bounty of Philadelphus. The king, wishing to laugh at his habit of verbal criticism, once told his treasurer to refuse his salary, and say that it had been already paid. Sosibius complained to the king, and the book of receipts was sent for, in which Philadelphus found the names of Soter, Sosigenes, Bion, and Apollonius, and showing to Sosibius one syllable of his name in each of those words, said that putting them together, they must be taken as the receipt for his salary.

Vitruvius,
lib. vii. præf. Among others who were brought to Alexandria by the fame of Philadelphus's bounty was Zoilus the grammarian, whose ill-natured criticism on Homer's poems had earned for him the name of Homeromastix, or *the scourge of Homer*. He read his criticisms to Philadelphus, who was so much displeased with his carping and unfair

manner of finding fault, that he even refused to relieve him when in distress. He told him that while thousands had earned a livelihood by pointing out the beauties of the Iliad and Odyssey in their public readings, surely one person who was so much wiser might be able to live by pointing out their faults.

Timon, a tragic poet, was also one of the visitors to this court; Diog. Laert. but, as Antigonus wittily said of him that he was fond of eating and drinking and sometimes at leisure for philosophy, we need not wonder at our knowing nothing of his tragedies, and at his not being made a professor by Philadelphus. But he took his revenge on the better-fed philosophers of the court, in a poem in which he Athenæus, lib. i. 19. calls them literary fighting-cocks, who were fattened by the king, and were always quarrelling in the coops of the Museum.

Such were the Greek authors who basked in the sunshine of royal favour at Alexandria; who could have told us, if they had thought it worth their while, all that we now wish to know of the trade, religion, language, and early history of Egypt. But they thought that the barbarians were not worth the notice of men who called themselves Macedonians. Philadelphus, however, thought otherwise; and by his command Manetho, an Egyptian priest of Syncellus. Heliopolis, wrote in Greek a history of Egypt, copied from the hieroglyphical writing on the temples, and dedicated to the king. We only know it in the quotations of other writers, and what we have is little more than a list of kings' names. Josephus quotes him as a pagan and therefore disinterested witness to the truth of the Jewish history; and, from the high value which we set upon every thing that throws light upon the Old Testament, nobody can read, without the deepest feelings of interest, the Egyptian, and therefore of course unfair, history of the Jews under Moses. The truth of Manetho's history, which runs back for nearly two thousand years, is shown by our finding the kings' names agree with every Egyptian inscription with which they can be compared.

Beside his history, Manetho has left us a work on astrology, called Apotelesmatica, or *Events,* a work of which there seems no reason to doubt the genuineness. It is a poem in hexameter verse, in good Greek, addressed to king Ptolemy, in which he calls, not only upon Apollo and the Muse, but, like a true Egyptian, upon Hermes, from whose darkly-worded writings he had gained his knowledge. He says that the king's greatness might have been foretold from the places of Mars and the Sun at the time of his birth, and that his marriage with his sister Arsinoë arose from the places of Venus and Saturn at the same time.

But while we smile at this being said as the result of astronomical calculations, we must remember that for centuries afterwards, almost in our own time, the science of judicial astrology was made a branch of astronomy, and that the fault lay rather in the age than in the man; and we have the pain of thinking that, while many of the valuable writings of Manetho are lost, the copiers and readers of manuscripts have carefully preserved this nearly worthless poem on astrology.

Manetho,
Apotelesm.

Petosiris was a writer on astronomy, who was highly praised by his friend Manetho, and whose calculations on the distances of the sun and planets are quoted by Pliny. His works are lost; but his name calls for our notice, as he must have been a native Egyptian, and a priest.

Lib. ii.

Strabo,
lib. ix. 421.

Timosthenes, the admiral of Philadelphus, must not be forgotten in this list of authors; for though his verses to Apollo were little worth notice, his voyages of discovery, and his work in ten books on harbours, placed him in the first rank among geographers.

But we must not only give Philadelphus credit for the learned and famous authors whom he brought to Alexandria, but also for those whom he sent for but could not get. Among these was Menander, the best of the Greek comic writers, whose works are still read with pleasure, over the whole world, in the translations of Terence. His speeches, in the opinion of Quinctilian, were alone enough to teach an orator every kind of eloquence. His power of invention and ease of dialogue were fitted for every passion and every situation of life, and threw all the other comic writers into the shade.

Philadelphus sent a ship to Athens on purpose to fetch him; but neither this honour nor the promised salary could make him quit his mother-country and the schools of Athens; and in the time of Pausanias his statue was still seen in the theatre, and his tomb still visited by the scholar on the road to the Piræus.

Pliny,
lib. vii. 31.

Colotes, a pupil and follower of Epicurus, dedicated to Philadelphus a work of which the very title proves the nature of his philosophy, and how soon the rules of his master had fitted themselves to the habits of the sensualist. Its title was, ' That no man need live according to the philosophical rules of another;' a looseness of principle which must at last be granted by everybody who, like Epicurus, makes happiness instead of goodness the end to be aimed at through life. It was a good deal read and talked about; and three hundred years afterwards Plutarch thought it not a waste of time to write against it at some length.

Plutarch.
in Colotem.

At a time when books were few, and far too dear to be within reach of the many, and indeed when the number of those who could read must have been small, other means were of course taken to meet the thirst after knowledge; and the chief of these were the public readings in the Theatre. This was not overlooked by Philadelphus, who employed Hegesias to read Herodotus, and Hermophantus to read Homer, the earliest historian and the earliest

Athenæus,
lib. xiv. 3.

poet, the two authors who had taken deepest root in the minds of the Greeks.

Plutarch. Aratus.

Philadelphus was not less fond of paintings and statues than of books; and he seems to have joined the Achaian league as much for the sake of the pictures which Aratus, its general, was in the habit of sending him, as for political reasons. Aratus, the chief of Sicyon, was an acknowledged judge of painting, and Sicyon was then the first school of Greece. The pieces which he sent to Philadelphus were mostly those of Pamphilus the master, and of Melanthius the fellow pupil, of Apelles.

Pliny, lib. xxxv. 36.

Pamphilus was famed for his perspective; and he is said to have received from every pupil the large sum of ten talents, or seventeen hundred pounds, a year. His best-known pieces were, Ulysses in his ship, the victory of the Athenians, and the battle of Phliuntes; but we are not told whether either of these were sent to Philadelphus. It was through Pamphilus that, at first in Sicyon and afterwards throughout all Greece, drawing was taught to boys as part of a liberal education.

lib. xxxv. 40.

Neacles also painted for Aratus; and we might almost suppose that it was as a gift to the king of Egypt that he painted his Sea-fight between the Egyptians and the Persians, in which the painter shows us that it was fought within the mouth of the Nile by making a crocodile bite at an ass drinking on the shore.

Ptolemæus, apud Photi-um.

Helena, the daughter of Timon, was a painter of great note at this time, at Alexandria; but the only piece of hers known to us by name is the battle of Issus, which three hundred years afterwards was hung up by Vespatian in the Temple of Peace at Rome. We must wonder at a woman choosing to paint the horrors and pains of a battle-piece; but, as we are not told what point of time was chosen, we may hope that it was after the battle, when Alexander, in his tent, raised up from their knees the wife and lovely daughter of Darius, who had been found among the prisoners.

We hear but little of the statues and sculptures made for Phila- delphus; but we cannot help remarking, that, while the public places of Athens were filled with the statues of the great and good men who had deserved well of their country, the statues which were most common in Alexandria were those of Cline, a favourite damsel, who filled the office of cup-bearer to the king.

Athenæus, lib. x. 7.

The favour shown to the Jews by Ptolemy Soter was not with- drawn by his son. He even bought and freed from slavery one hundred and twenty thousand men of that nation, who were scat- tered over Egypt. He paid for each, out of the royal treasury, one hundred and twenty drachmas, or about three pounds ten shillings, to those of his subjects who held them either by right of war or by purchase. The Jews who lived in Lower Egypt, in the full enjoyment of civil and religious liberty, looked upon that country as their home. They had already a Greek translation of either the whole or some part of their sacred writings, which had been made for those whose families had been for so many generations in Egypt, that they could not read the language of their forefathers. But they now hoped by means of the king's friendship, and the weight which his wishes must carry with them, to have a Greek trans- lation of the Bible which should bear the stamp of authority.

Josephus, Antiq. xii. 2.

Accordingly, to please them Philadelphus sent Aristæus, a man whose wisdom had gained his friendship, and Andræus a captain of the guard, both of them Greek Jews, with costly gifts to Eleazer the high priest of Jerusalem; and asked him to employ learned and fit men to make a Greek translation of the Bible for the library at Alexandria. Eleazar named seventy elders to undertake the task, who held their first sitting on the business at the king's dinner-

Diog. Laert. table; when Menedemus the Socratic philosopher, the pupil of Plato, was also present, who had been sent to Philadelphus as ambassador from Euboea. The translators then divided the work among themselves; and when each had finished his task it was laid before a meeting of the seventy, and then published by authority. Thus was made the whole or part of the Greek translation of the Old Testament, which, from the number of the translators, we now call the Septuagint.

Plutarch.
Aratus. When Aratus of Sicyon first laid a plot to free his country from its tyrant, he sent to Philadelphus for help in money; but the king seems to have thought the plans of this young man too wild to be countenanced. Aratus however soon raised his state to a level with the first states of Greece, and made himself leader of the Achaian league, under which band and name the Greeks were then struggling for freedom against the great surrounding kingdoms; and when by his courage and success he had shown himself worthy of the proud name which was afterwards given him—of the last of the Greeks, Philadelphus, like other patrons, gave him the help which he less needed. Aratus, as we have seen, bought his friendship with pictures, the gifts of all others the most welcome; and, when he went to Egypt, Philadelphus gave him one hundred and fifty talents or twenty-five thousand pounds, and joined the Achaian league, on the agreement that he was to direct the war by sea and land.

The friendship of Philadelphus, indeed, was courted by all the Pausanias,
lib. i. 6.
Inscript.
Letronne,
Recherches. neighbouring states; the Athenians named one of the tribes of their city by his name; the little island of Delos set up its statue to him; and the cities of Greece vied with one another in doing him honour.

He had, when young, married Arsinoë the daughter of Lysimachus of Thrace, by whom he had three children, Ptolemy, who succeeded him, Lysimachus, and Berenice ; but having found that his wife was intriguing with Amyntas, and with Crysippus a physician of Rhodes, he put these two to death, and banished Arsinoë to Coptos in the Thebaid.

Scholiast. in Theocrito, xvii. 128.

He then took Arsinoë his own sister as the partner of his throne. She had married first the old Lysimachus king of Thrace, and then Ceraunus her half-brother, when he was king of Macedonia. As they were not children of the same mother, this second marriage was neither illegal nor improper in Macedonia ; but her third marriage with Philadelphus could only be justified by the laws of Egypt, their adopted country. They were both past the middle age, and whether Philadelphus looked upon her as his wife or not, at any rate they had no children. Her own children by Lysimachus had been put to death by Ceraunus, and she readily adopted those of her brother with all the kindness of a mother.

She was a woman of an enlarged mind ; her husband and her step-children alike valued her; and Eratosthenes showed his opinion of her learning and strong sense by giving the name of Arsinoë to one of his works, which perhaps a modern writer would have named Table-talk.

Athenæus, lib. vii. 1.

This marriage, however, did not escape blame with the Greeks of Alexandria ; and the poet Sotades, whose verses were as licentious as his life, having written some coarse lines against the queen, was forced to fly from Egypt, but being overtaken at sea he was wrapt up in lead and thrown overboard.

lib. xiv. 4.

In the Egyptian inscriptions Ptolemy and Arsinoë are always called the Brother-gods ; on the coins they are called Adelphi, *the brothers ;* and afterwards the king took the name of Philadelphus or *sister-loving,* by which he is now usually known.

In the first half of his reign Philadelphus dated his coins from the year that his father came to the throne; and it was not till the nineteenth year of his reign, soon after the death of his mother, that he made an era of his own, and dated his coins by the year of his own reign. Among them is one with the heads of Soter and Philadelphus on the one side, and the head of Berenice, the wife of the one and mother of the other, on the other side. This we may suppose to have been struck during the first two years of his reign, in the lifetime of his father.

Visconti, Icon. Grec.

Another bears on one side the heads of Ptolemy Soter and Berenice, with the word ΘΕΩΝ, ' *of the gods*,' and on the other side the heads of Philadelphus and his second wife Arsinoë, with the word ΑΔΕΛΦΩΝ, ' *of the brothers*.'

A third was struck by the king in honour of his queen and sister. On the one side is the head of the queen, with the words ΑΡΣΙΝΟΗΣ ΦΙΛΑΔΕΛΦΟΥ, ' *of Arsinoë the brother-loving*,' and on the other is the double cornucopia.

Pliny, lib. xxxvi. 14.

On the death of Arsinoë he built a tomb for her in Alexandria, called the Arsinoëum; in which he set up an obelisk eighty cubits high, which had been made by king Nectanebo, but had been left plain, without carving. Satyrus the architect had the charge of moving it. He is said to have dug a canal to it as it lay upon the ground, and to have moved two heavily laden barges under it. The burdens were then taken out of the barges, and as they floated higher they raised the obelisk off the ground. He then found it a task as great or greater to set it up in its place; and this Greek engineer must surely have looked back with wonder on the labour and knowledge of mechanics which must have been used in setting up the obelisks, colossal statues, and pyramids, which he saw scattered over the country.

As a further honour to his sister, Philadelphus is said to have lib. xxxiv. 42. listened to the whimsical proposal of Dinochares the architect, to build a room of load-stone, in her tomb; so that an iron statue of the queen should hang in the air between the floor and the roof. But the death of the king and of the architect took place before this was tried.

Philadelphus lived in peace with Ergamenes king of Meroë, Diod. Sic. lib. iii. 6. who, while seeking for a knowledge of philosophy and the arts of life from his Greek neighbours, seems also to have gained a love of despotism, and a dislike of that control with which the priests of Ethiopia and Egypt had always limited the power of their kings. Accordingly he surrounded the golden temple with a chosen body of troops, and put the whole of the priests to death; and from that time he governed Ethiopia as an autocrat. But with the loss of their liberties the Ethiopians lost the wish and power to guard the throne; and in the next reign their country was conquered by Egypt.

The wars between Philadelphus and his great neighbour Antio- Hieronymus, in Dan. xi. chus Theos seem not to have been carried on very actively, though they did not wholly cease, till Philadelphus offered as a bribe his daughter Berenice, with a large sum of money under the name of a dower. Antiochus was already married to Laodice, whom he loved dearly, and by whom he had two children, Seleucus and Antiochus; but, notwithstanding this, he agreed to declare this first marriage void, and his two sons illegitimate, and that his children, if any should be born to him by Berenice, should inherit the throne of Babylon and the east. Philadelphus led his daughter to Pelusium, on her journey to her betrothed husband, and sent with her so large a sum of gold and silver that he was nicknamed the dower-giver.

Libanius,
Orat. xi.

The peace between the two countries lasted as long as Philadel-phus lived, and was strengthened by kindnesses which each did to the other.　Ptolemy, when in Syria, was much struck by the beauty of a statue of Diana, and begged it of Antiochus as an ornament for Alexandria.　But as soon as the statue reached Egypt Arsinoë fell dangerously ill, and she dreamed that the goddess came to her by night, and told her that the illness was sent to her for the wrong done to the statue by her husband; and accordingly the statue was sent back with many gifts to the temple.

Pliny,
lib. vii. 37.

Antiochus, when ill, sent to Alexandria for a physician, and Cleombrotus of Cos was sent to Syria.　He was successful in curing the king, and on his return he received from Philadelphus a present of one hundred talents, or seventeen thousand pounds, as a fee for his journey.

lib. xxix. 2, 3.

Suidas.

Erasistratus of Cos also had the credit of having once cured Antiochus.　He was the grandson of Aristotle, and held high rank as a physician, and may even be called the father of the science of anatomy: his writings are often quoted by Dioscorides.　Antio-chus in his youth had fallen deeply in love with his young step-mother, and was pining away in silence and despair.　Erasistratus found out the cause of his illness, which was straightway cured by Seleucus giving up his wife to his own son.　This act strongly points out the changed opinions of the world in matters of right and wrong; for it was then thought the father's best title to the name of Nicanor; he had before conquered his enemies, but he then conquered himself.

Erasistratus was the first who thought that a knowledge of ana-tomy should be made a part of the healing art.　Before his time surgery and medicine had been deemed one and the same; they had both been studied by the slow and uncertain steps of experience unguided by theory. Every man who had been ill, whether through disease or wound, and had regained his health, thought it his duty to the god and his neighbours to write up in the temple of Esculapius the nature of his ailings and the simples to which he fancied that he owed his cure. By copying these loose but well-meant inscriptions of medical cases, Hippocrates had, a century before, laid the foundations of the science; but nothing further was added to it till Erasistratus, setting at nought the prejudices of the Greeks, began dissecting the human body in the schools of Alexandria.

Herophilus lived about the same time with Erasistratus, and was like him famous for his knowledge of the anatomy of man. But so hateful was this study in the eyes of the Greeks, that these anatomists were charged, by writers who ought to have known better, with the cruelty of cutting men open when alive.

Celsus, lib. i.

They had few followers in the hated use of the dissecting knife. It was from their writings that Galen borrowed the anatomical parts of his work; and thus it was to the dissections of these two great men, helped indeed by opening the bodies of animals, that the world owed almost the whole of its knowledge of the anatomy of man, till the fifteenth century, when surgeons were again bold enough to face the outcry of the mob, and to study the human body with the knife.

Philadelphus, though a lover of learning beyond other kings of his time, also surpassed them in his unmeasured luxury and love of pleasure. He had many mistresses, Egyptian as well as Greek, and the names of some of them have been handed down to us. He often boasted that he had found out the way to live for ever; but, like other free-livers, he was sometimes, by the gout in his feet, made to acknowledge that he was only a man, and indeed

Athenæus, lib. xiii. 5.

lib. xii. 9.

to wish that he could change places with the beggar whom he saw from his palace windows, eating the refuse on the banks of the Nile with an appetite which he had long wanted.

Theocritus,
Id. xvii.

He reigned over Egypt, with the neighbouring parts of Arabia; also over Libya, Phenicia, Cœlo-Syria, part of Ethiopia, Pamphylia, Cilicia, Lycia, Caria, Cyprus, and the isles of the Cyclades. The island of Rhodes, and many of the cities of Greece, were bound to him by the closest ties of friendship, for past help and for the hope of future. The forces of Egypt reached the very large number of

Hieronymus,
in Dan. xi.

two hundred thousand foot and twenty thousand horse, two thousand chariots, four hundred Ethiopian elephants, fifteen hundred ships of war, and one thousand transports. Of this large force, it is not likely that even one fourth should have been Greeks; the rest must have been Egyptians and Syrians, with some Gauls; all of whom, though now armed and disciplined like Greeks, were very much below the Macedonian phalanx in real strength. The galleys, also, though no doubt under the guidance and skill of Greeks and Phenicians, were in part manned by Egyptians, whose inland habits wholly unfitted them for the sea, and whose religious prejudices made them feel the pressing for the navy as a heavy grievance.

These large forces were maintained by a yearly income, equally large, of fourteen thousand eight hundred talents, or two millions and a half pounds sterling, beside the tax on corn, which was taken in kind, of a million and a half of artabas, or about five millions of

Appian.
Præf. 10.

bushels. To this we may add a mass of gold, silver, and other valuable stores in the treasury, which were reckoned at the unheard-of sum of seven hundred and forty thousand talents, or above one hundred million pounds sterling.

The trade down the Nile was larger than it had ever been before;

the coasting trade on the Mediterranean was wholly new; the people were rich and happy; justice was administered to the Egyptians according to their own laws, and to the Greeks of Alexandria according to the Macedonian laws; the navy commanded the whole of the eastern half of the Mediterranean; the schools and library had risen to a great height upon the wise plans of Ptolemy Soter; in every point of view Alexandria was the chief city in the world. Philadelphus, by joining to the greatness and good government of his father the costly splendour and pomp of an eastern monarch, so drew the eyes of after ages upon his reign, that his name passed into a proverb: if any work of art was remarkable for its good taste or costliness, it was called Philadelphian; even history and chronology were set at nought, and we sometimes find poets of a century later counted among the Pleiades of Alexandria in the reign of Philadelphus.

Philo Judæus, de Mose.

It is true that many of these advantages were forced in the hot-bed of royal patronage; that the navy was built in the harbours of Palestine; and that the men of letters who then drew upon themselves the eyes of the world were only Greek settlers, whose writings could have done little to raise the character of the native Copts. But the Ptolemies, in raising this building of their own, were not at the same time crushing another. Their splendid monarchy had not been built on the ruins of freedom; and even if the Greek settlers in the Delta had formed themselves into a free state, we can hardly believe that the Egyptians would have been so well treated as they were by this military despotism. From the temples which were built or enlarged in Upper Egypt, and from the beauty of the hieroglyphical inscriptions, we find that even the native arts were more flourishing than they had ever been since the fall of the kings of Thebes, and we may almost look upon the conquest of Egypt by the Greeks, and its remaining under the Ptolemies, as a blessing to the people of Upper Egypt.

Porphyrius,
ap. Scalig. Philadelphus died in the thirty-eighth year of his reign, leaving the kingdom as powerful and more wealthy than when it came to him from his father; and he had the happiness of having a son who would carry on, even for the third generation, the wise and good plans of the first Ptolemy.

PTOLEMY EUERGETES.

No sooner was Philadelphus dead, than Antiochus, who had married Berenice only because it was one of the articles of the treaty
with Egypt, sent her away with her young son. He then recalled
his first wife Laodice, who, distrusting her changeable husband, had
him at once murdered to secure the throne to her own children.
Seleucus, the eldest, seized the throne of Syria; and, urged on by
his mother, sent a body of men after Berenice, with orders to put
her to death, together with her son, who by the articles of marriage
had been made heir to the throne.

The cities of Asia Minor hastily sent help to the queen and her
son, while Ptolemy Euergetes, her brother, marched without loss
of time into Syria. But it was too late to save them: they were
both put to death by the soldiers of Seleucus.

Many of the states of Asia Minor, moved by hatred of their king's
cruelty, opened their gates to the army of Euergetes; and, had he
not been recalled to Egypt by troubles at home, he would soon have
been master of the whole of the kingdom of Seleucus. As it was,
he had marched beyond the Euphrates, had left an Egyptian army
in Seleucia, the capital of Syria, and had gained a large part of Asia
Minor. On his march homeward, he laid his gifts upon the altar
in the temple of Jerusalem, and returned thanks to Heaven for his
victories. He had been taught to bow the knee to the crowds of
Greek and Egyptian gods; and, as Palestine was part of his kingdom, it seemed quite natural to add the god of the Jews to the list.

Justinus,
lib. xxvii. 1.
B.C. 246.

Hieronymus,
in Dan. xi.

Josephus,
in Apion. ii.

Callimachus, ap. Catullum.

It was while the king was from home upon this Assyrian war, that his queen Berenice, sacrificing a bull to the gods, vowed that, if they brought her husband safe home, she would cut off her beautiful tresses, and hang them up in the temple in token of her thankfulness. Euergetes soon afterwards returned a conqueror, and the queen's locks were yielded up to the knife, while the whole court praised her heroism.

Conon the astronomer was then busy in noting the places of the fixed stars, and immediately grouping together into a constellation one of those many clusters which the earlier astronomers had left unnamed, he marked it out on his globe and gave it to the world as the new constellation of the Hair of Berenice. Callimachus took the hint from the courtly astronomer, and, in a poem which we know only in the translation of Catullus, makes the hair swear by the head from which it was cut off, that it was against its will that it left the queen, and was raised to the skies; but what could it do against the force of steel? The poet and the astronomer have here been of use to one another; the constellation of Coma Berenices is known to hundreds who have not read Callimachus or Catullus, but it is from the poet that we learn why it was set among the stars.

Justinus, lib. xxvii. 2.

No sooner had Euergetes reached home than Seleucus, in his turn, marched upon Egypt, and sent for his brother Antiochus Hierax, to bring up his forces and to join him. But before Antiochus could come up, the army of Seleucus was already beaten; and Antiochus, instead of helping his brother in his distress, strove to rob him of his crown. Instead of leading his army against Euergetes, he marched upon Seleucus, and by the help of his Gallic mercenaries beat him in battle. But the traitor was himself soon afterwards beaten by Eumenes king of Bithynia, who had entered

Syria in the hope that it would fall an easy prey into his hands after being torn to pieces by civil war.

Antiochus, after the rout of his army, fled to Egypt, believing that he should meet with kinder treatment from Euergetes, his enemy, than after his late treachery he could hope for from his own brother. But he was ordered by Euergetes to be closely guarded, and when he afterwards made his escape he lost his life in his flight by unknown hands.

The Romans, on hearing of the war, sent to Egypt with friendly offers of help, but the war was over by the time that their ambassadors reached Alexandria, and they were sent home with thanks.

Eutropius, lib. iii. 1.
B.C. 238.

The king, in his attack upon Seleucus, carried off a large booty of forty thousand talents of silver, and, what he seems to have valued even more than that treasure, two thousand five hundred vases and statues of the gods; many of which either really were, or were said to be, those carried away from Egypt by Cambyses nearly three hundred years before. These were replaced in the temples of Upper Egypt with great pomp; and the priests, in gratitude for the care which he had thus shown for the religion and the temples of the country, then gave him the name of Euergetes, or *the bene-factor*.

Hieronymus, in Dan. xi.

In Alexander the Egyptians had seen a deliverer from the Persian yoke, and a humane conqueror, who left them their customs and their religion. In Ptolemy Soter they had a brave and just king who kept war at a distance, and by his wise laws laid the foundation of the future greatness of his family, of Alexandria, and of his kingdom. In Philadelphus they had also a Greek king whose love of learning and of show dazzled the eyes of the people, and whose court at Alexandria had carried away from Athens the honour of being the favoured seat of the muses. But Euergetes was a native Egyptian, and though perhaps the least of these great kings, in the eyes of the priests he must have ranked at their head. He seems to have thought more of conquering Ethiopia than Assyria; he was the only one of the Ptolemies who is known to have honoured the once great city of Thebes with a visit; he enriched the temples, and sacrificed to the gods of the country, not through policy but through choice; and when, during the minority of his grandson, the priests and temples were again flourishing, they showed their gratitude by saying that the young king had acted in obedience to the will of the god Euergetes.

Rosetta Stone.

Wilkinson's
Thebes.

Euergetes enlarged the great temple at Thebes, which is now called the temple of Karnak, on the walls of which we see him handing an offering to his father and mother the Brother-gods. In one place he is in a Greek dress, which is not common on the Ptolemaic buildings, as most of the Greek kings are carved upon the walls in the dress of the country. He added to the temple at Hibe in the great oasis, and began a small temple at Esne, or Latopolis, where he is drawn upon the walls in the act of striking down the chiefs of the conquered nations, and is followed by a tame lion.

Inscript.
Letronne,
Recherches.

He built a temple to Osiris at Canopus, on the mouth of the Nile, for, notwithstanding the large number of Greeks and strangers which had settled there, the ancient religion was not yet driven out of the Delta; and he dedicated it to the god in a Greek inscription on a plate of gold, in the names of himself and Berenice, whom he called his wife and sister. She is also called the king's sister in many of the hieroglyphical inscriptions, as are many of the other queens of the Ptolemies who were not so related to their husbands. This custom, though it took its rise in the Egyptian mythology, must have been strengthened by the marriages of Philadelphus and some of his successors with their sisters.

In the hieroglyphical inscriptions he is usually called ' beloved by Pthah,' the god of Memphis, an addition to his name which was used by most of his successors.

Hieroglyphics seem to have flourished in their more ancient style and forms under the generous patronage of the Ptolemies. In the time of the Egyptian kings of Lower Egypt, we find new grammatical endings to the nouns, and more letters used to spell each word than under the kings of Thebes ; but on comparing the hieroglyphics of the Ptolemies with the others, we find that in these and some other points they are more like the older writings, under the kings of Thebes, than the newer, under the kings of Sais.

But while the Egyptians were flattered and no doubt raised in moral worth by their monarch's taking up the religious feelings of the country, and throwing aside some of the Greek habits of his father and grandfather, Euergetes was sowing the seeds of a greater change than he could have been himself aware of. It was by Greek arms and arts of war that Egypt then held its place among nations, and we shall see in the coming reigns, that while the court became more Asiatic and less European, the army and government did not remain unchanged.

Euergetes, finding himself at peace with all his neighbours on the coasts of the Mediterranean, then turned his arms towards the south. He easily conquered the tribes of Ethiopia, whose wild courage could set no barrier to the arms and discipline of the Greek mercenaries ; and at Adule, a port on the Red Sea, in latitude 15°, he set up a large chair or throne of white marble, on which he recounted his victories in a Greek inscription.

Cosmas Indicopleustes.

We ought not perhaps to feel sure that the inscription on the base of this chair was written by the same king, because it is dated in the twenty-seventh year of his reign, while Euergetes seems only to have reigned twenty-five years; and because the first half of the inscription on the chair is in the third person, while the second half, on the base, speaks in the first: but it adds, that he stretched his march to the foot of the snowy mountains in which the Nile rises, and conquered the frankincense country on the borders of the desert plains of central Africa: that from these tribes he brought away a large booty of slaves and treasure, but was more often content with their acknowledging his sovereignty and promising a yearly tribute, which they may have promised the more readily as he left no forces to collect it: that he then carried his foot soldiers across the Red Sea, and conquered the Arabs and Sabæans, and made their kings promise, not only a yearly tribute, but what was even of more value, a free passage by land and sea for the traders through their country.

For a copy of this curious inscription, usually called the *Monumentum Adulitanum*, we are indebted to Cosmas, a merchant of Alexandria, who traded to India in the beginning of the sixth century. He was one of those remarkable men, who, rising above the crowd, and joining letters to trade in an age when very few of his class were authors, wrote as a scholar while he travelled as a merchant. He is usually known by the name of Cosmas Indicopleustes, or *the Indian navigator*.

Josephus,
Antiq. xii. 3. In the latter end of this reign Onias, the high-priest of Jerusalem, a weak and covetous old man, refused to send to Alexandria the yearly tribute from the Temple, of twenty talents, or three thousand four hundred pounds. When Euergetes sent to claim it, and even threatened to send a body of troops to fetch it, still the tribute was not sent; notwithstanding the fright of the Jews, the priest would not part with his money.

On this, Joseph the nephew of Onias set out for Egypt, to try and turn away the king's anger, and he made himself so agreeable that he was lodged in the palace at Memphis, and dined every day with the king. While he was there the revenues of the provinces for the coming year were put up to auction, and the farmers bid eight thousand talents, or one million four hundred thousand pounds, for the taxes of Cœlo-Syria, Phenicia, and Samaria. Joseph then bid double that sum, and when he was asked what security he could give, he playfully said that he was sure that Euergetes and the queen would willingly become bound for his honesty; and the king was so much pleased with him, that the office was at once given to him, and he held it for twenty-two years.

Euergetes did not forget his allies in Greece, but continued the yearly payment to Aratus the general of the Achaian league; and when the Spartans under Cleomenes tried to overthrow the power of the Achaians, Euergetes would not help them. He naturally thought that they wished to throw off their dependance on Alexandria, and he might perhaps have had the wisdom to see that if the Grecian states quarrelled among themselves they could no longer withstand the armies of Syria.

Plutarch. Cleomenes.

But Cleomenes, while struggling to raise his little kingdom to its former rank among the states of Greece, was not so unwise as to break the Egyptian treaty, and to throw himself into the power of his more dangerous neighbour the king of Syria; and, when Antigonus marched upon the Peloponnesus, Cleomenes routed his army at the Isthmus of Corinth. Antigonus, however, afterwards passed the isthmus, and beat the Spartans before the walls of Argos.

Cleomenes then sent to Egypt for help in money; but the distrust of Euergetes was not wholly removed, and the money was not granted till he had sent his mother and children to Alexandria, as hostages for his good faith. With the gold of Egypt he raised an army of twenty thousand men; but he was soon afterwards beaten at Sellasia by Antigonus with thirty thousand, and the whole of the Peloponnesus, weakened by the jealousy of its states, then fell under the power of the Syrians. Upon this, Cleomenes sailed for Alexandria, where he was kindly received by Euergetes, who then saw how mistaken he had been in distrusting this brave Spartan, and gave him twenty-four talents or four thousand pounds a-year for his maintenance in Egypt, till he should be sent back to Greece with a fleet and army to regain his throne.

Suidas.

Among the men of letters who at this time lived and taught in the schools of Alexandria, was Aristophanes the grammarian, who gained the high office of head of the Museum in a very remark-

Vitruvius, lib. vii. præf.

able way. At one of the public sittings at which the king was to hear the poems and other writings of the pupils read, and, by the help of seven men of letters who sat with him as judges, was to give away honours and rewards to the best authors, one of the chairs was empty—one of the judges happened not to be there. The king asked who should be called up to fill his place; and, after thinking over the matter, the six judges fixed upon Aristophanes, who had made himself known to them by being seen daily reading in the public library. When the reading was over, the king, the public, and the six other judges were agreed upon which was the best piece of writing; but Aristophanes was bold enough to think otherwise, and he was able by means of his great reading to find the very book in the library from which the pupil had copied the greater part of his work. The king was much struck with this proof of his learning, and soon afterwards made him keeper of the library.

Pliny, lib. vi. 34.

Eratosthenes, the inventor of astronomical geography, was at this time at the head of the mathematical school. He was the first who fixed the place of a city upon the earth by the help of astronomy, or by means of its latitude, which he learnt from the length of the sun's shadow at noon on the equinoctial days; and he named this observation the Theory of Shadows. From this he found that the earth was a ball; and, by measuring the distance between two places, he learnt the length of a degree of latitude, which he found to be seven hundred stadia, and that three hundred and sixty times that distance, or two hundred and fifty-two thousand stadia, was the measure of the earth's circumference. Strabo, lib. i.

With this knowledge, he lessened the mistakes in maps, which before his time had been drawn without any help from astronomy, and in which the distances in miles had been mostly laid down by days' journeys, or by measuring along the crooked roads. By these great strides of science, he justly earned the name of Surveyor of the World.

By measuring the sun's shadow, at a place, on the longest and on the shortest day in the year, he learned the obliquity of the ecliptic, which he fixed at more than 23° 50′, and less than 23° 52′ 30″. But in pure mathematics he did not rank so high. Hipparchus said that he wrote mathematically about geography, and geographically about mathematics: indeed Hipparchus, in his Commentaries on the Geography of Eratosthenes, in many places defended the old maps against his too bold changes. Ptolemy, lib. i. Strabo, lib. i.

He was a man of such unbounded knowledge, and so nearly at the head of every branch of science, that, as in philosophy he was called a *second* Plato, and was spoken of in the same way in many other sciences, he was jokingly called Beta, or Number Two.

His longest work now remaining is a description of the constellations. He also wrote a history of Egypt, to correct the errors of Manetho; but, by comparing the two with the hieroglyphical monuments from which they were each taken, we can well understand how the boldness of Eratosthenes sometimes called down the blame of Hipparchus, 'the lover of truth.' But nevertheless his history is of great use to us; for, while Manetho's lists only give us the separate dynasties of the several cities, without saying which king reigned over all Egypt, and which was under the sceptre of another, Eratosthenes has given us a straightforward list of the kings of Thebes, without separating them into dynasties.

But what most strikes us with wonder and regret is, that these two writers,—Manetho, an Egyptian priest who wrote in Greek; Eratosthenes, a Greek who understood Egyptian,—neither of them took the trouble to lay open to their readers the peculiarities of the hieroglyphics. Through all these reigns, the titles and praises of the Ptolemies were carved upon the temples in the sacred characters. These two histories were translated from the same inscriptions. We even now read the names of the kings which they mention carved on the granite temples and statues; and yet the language of the hieroglyphics still remained unknown beyond the class of priests; such was the want of curiosity on the part of the Greek grammarians of Alexandria.

Diog. Laert. Lycon of Troas succeeded Strato, whom we have before spoken of, at the head of one of the schools in the Museum. He was very successful in bringing up the young men, who needed, he used to say, modesty and the love of praise, as a horse needs bridle and spur. His eloquence was so pleasing that he was wittily called Glycon, or *the sweet.*

Suidas. Apollonius, who was born at Alexandria, but is commonly called Apollonius Rhodius because he passed many years of his life at Rhodes, had been, like Eratosthenes, a hearer of Callimachus. His only work which we now know is his Argonautics, a poem on the voyage of Jason to Colchis in search of the golden fleece. It is a regular epic poem, in imitation of Homer, and, like other imitations, it wants the interest which hangs upon reality of manners and story in the Iliad. Aristophanes, and his pupil Aristarchus, the great critics of the day, with whose judgement few dared to differ, and who had perhaps quarrelled with the poet, declared that it was not poetry; and after that, the most that Quintilian would say for it was, that it ought not to be overlooked, for it never falls below mediocrity. Quintilian, lib. x. 1.

His master Callimachus showed his dislike of his young rival by hurling against him a reproachful poem, in which he speaks of him under the name of an Ibis. This is now lost, but it was copied by Ovid in his poem of the same name; and from the Roman we can gather something of the dark and learned style in which Callimachus threw out his biting reproaches. We do not know from what this quarrel arose, but it seems to have been the cause of Apollonius leaving Alexandria. He removed to Rhodes, where he taught eloquence during all the reign of Philopator, till he was recalled by Epiphanes, and made librarian of the Museum in his old age, on the death of Eratosthenes. Suidas. Callimachus.

Many of the old philosophers were fond of clothing wisdom in the dress of proverbs, or short sentences; and one by Apollonius has been handed down to us, which, though prettily worded, we must fear was meant ill-naturedly. He said that 'nothing dries sooner than a tear.' Cicero, de Inventione, lib. i.

Lycophron, the tragic writer, lived about this time at Alexandria, and was one of the seven men of letters sometimes called the Alexandrian Pleiades, though writers are not agreed upon the names which fill up the list. His tragedies are all lost, and the only work of his which we now have is the dark and muddy poem of Alcandra, Suidas.

or Cassandra, of which the lines most striking to the historian are those in which the prophetess foretells the coming greatness of Rome; 'that the children of Æneas will raise the crown upon their spears, and seize the sceptres of sea and land.' Lycophron was the friend of Menedemus and Aratus; but, as it is not easy to believe that these lines were written before the overthrow of Hannibal in Italy, and of the Greek phalanx in Cynocephalæ, he may have been a young man in the reign of Philadelphus, and yet have seen the triumph of the Roman arms.

Line 1227.
Diog. Laert.

Old Testam.
Apocrypha.

In this list of Alexandrian authors, we must not forget to mention Jesus the son of Sirach, who came into Egypt in this reign, and translated into Greek the Hebrew writings of his grandfather Jesus, which are named the Book of Ecclesiasticus. It is written in imitation of the Proverbs of Solomon; and though its pithy sayings fall far short of the deep wisdom and lofty thoughts which crowd every line of that wonderful work, yet it will always be read with profit and pleasure.

Apollonius of Perga came to Alexandria in this reign, to study mathematics under the pupils of Euclid. He is well known for his writings on conic sections, or the several curves which are made by cutting a cone; and he may be called the founder of this study. The properties of the ellipse, the hyperbola, and the parabola continued to be studied by after mathematicians; but still it may be said to have been an unrewarded study till nearly two thousand years later, when Kepler crowned the labours of Apollonius with the great discovery that the paths of the planets round the sun were conic sections.

But while we are dazzled by the brilliancy of the clusters of men of letters and science who graced the court of Alexandria, we must not shut our eyes to those faults which must always be found in works called forth rather by the fostering warmth of royal pensions than by a love of knowledge in the people. The well-fed and well-paid philosophers of the Museum were not likely to overtake the mighty men of Athens, who had studied and taught without any pension from the government, without taking any fee from their pupils; who were urged forward only by the love of knowledge and of honour; who had no other aim than that of being useful to their hearers, and looked for no reward beyond their love and esteem.

Books may, if we please, be divided into works of industry and works of taste. Among the first we may place mathematics, criticism, and compilations; among the second we ought to find poetry and oratory. Works of industry and care may be found in many ages and in many countries, but those which have gained the praises of all mankind, for their pure taste and fire of genius, seem to have ripened only on those spots and in those times at which the mind of man, from causes perhaps too deep for our search, has been able to burst forth with more than usual strength.

When we review the writings of the authors of Alexandria, we are forced to acknowledge that they are most of them of the former class; we may say of them all, what Ovid said of Callimachus, that they are more to be admired for their industry and art than for their taste and genius; most of the poets and orators are forgotten, while we even now look back to Alexandria as the cradle of geometry, geography, astronomy, anatomy, and criticism. *Amor. i. 15.*

The coins of Euergetes bear the words ΠΤΟΛΕΜΑΙΟΤ ΒΑΣΙΛΕΩΣ, *Visconti, Icon. Grec.* 'of Ptolemy the king,' round the head on the one side, with no title by which they can be known from the other kings of the same name. But his portrait is known from his Phenician coins, as none but the first five Ptolemies could have coined in Phenicia, and the likenesses of the other four of them are well known.

In the same way the coins of his queen Berenice have only the words ΒΕΡΕΝΙΚΗΣ ΒΑΣΙΛΙΣΣΗΣ ; ' *of Berenice the queen,*' but they are known from those of the later queens by the beauty of their workmanship, which soon fell far below that of the first Ptolemies.

Euergetes had married his cousin Berenice, who like the other queens of Egypt is sometimes called Cleopatra ; by her he left two sons, Ptolemy and Magas, to the eldest of whom he left his king-dom, after a reign of twenty-five years of unclouded prosperity.

Porphyrius, ap. Scalig.

Egypt was during this reign at the very height of its power and wealth. It had seen three kings, who, though not equally great men, not equally fit to found a monarchy or to raise the literature of a people, were equally successful in the parts which they had undertaken. Euergetes left to his son a kingdom, perhaps as large as the world had ever seen under one sceptre, and though many of his boasted victories were like letters written in the sand, of which the traces were soon lost, yet he was by far the greatest monarch of his day.

We may be sure that in these prosperous reigns life and property were safe, and justice was administered fairly by judges who were independent of the crown; as even centuries afterwards we find that it was part of a judge's oath on taking office, that if he were ordered by the king to do what was wrong, he would not obey him.

Plutarch. Apophthegm.

But here the bright pages of Egyptian history end. Though trade and agriculture still enriched the country, though arts and letters did not quit Alexandria in an instant, we have from this time forward to mark the growth of only vice and luxury, and to measure the wisdom of Ptolemy Soter by the length of time that his laws and institutions were able to bear up against misrule and folly.

PTOLEMY PHILOPATOR.

THE first act of the new king was to call together his council, and to ask their advice about putting to death his mother Berenice and his brother Magas. Their crime was being too much liked by the army, and the council was called upon to say whether it would be safe to have them killed. Cleomenes, the banished king of Sparta, who was one of the council, alone raised his voice against their murder, and said that the throne would be still safer if there were more brothers to stand between the king and the daring hopes of a traitor. The minister Sosibius said that the mercenaries could not be trusted while Magas was alive, but Cleomenes remarked to him, that more than three thousand of them were Peloponnesians, and that they would follow him sooner than they would Magas.

Berenice and Magas were however put to death, but the speech of Cleomenes was not forgotten. If his popularity with the mercenaries could secure their allegiance, he could, when he chose, make them rebel: and from that time he was treated rather as a prisoner than as a friend, and he lost all chance of being helped to regain his kingdom.

Nothing is known of the death of Euergetes, the late king, and there is no proof that it was by unfair means. But when his son began a cruel and wicked reign by putting to death his mother and brother, and by taking the name of Philopator, or *father-loving*, the world seems to have thought that he was the murderer of his father, and had taken this name to throw a cloak over the deed.

Plutarch.
Cleomenes.
Polybius,
lib. v.
B.C. 221.

Polybius,
lib. v.

The task of the historian would be more agreeable if he always had to point out how crime and goodness were followed by their just rewards; but unfortunately history is not free from acts of successful wickedness. By the murder of his brother, and by the minority both of Antiochus king of Syria, and of Philip king of Macedonia, Philopator found himself free from enemies either at home or abroad, and he gave himself up to a life of thoughtlessness and pleasure. The army and fleet were left to go to ruin, and the foreign provinces, which his wise forefathers had looked upon as the bulwarks of Egypt, were only half guarded: but the throne rested on the virtues of his forefathers, and it was not till his death that it was found to have been undermined by his own vices.

Egypt had been governed by kings of more than usual wisdom for above one hundred years, and was at the very height of its power when Philopator came to the throne. He found himself master of Ethiopia, Cyrene, Phenicia, Cœlo-Syria, part of Upper Syria, Cyprus, Rhodes, the cities along the coast of Asia Minor from Pamphylia to Lysimachia, and the cities of Ænos and Maronea in Thrace. Egypt was the greatest naval power in the world, having the command of the sea and the whole of the coast of the eastern end of the Mediterranean.

But on the death of Euergetes the happiness of the people came to an end. In a despotic monarchy, where so much rests upon the good qualities of the king, we can hardly hope to find a longer course of good government than we have seen at Alexandria. The flatterers and pleasures which are brought to the court by the greatness and wealth of each king in his turn, must at last poison the heart and turn the head of a son; and thus it was with Philopator.

The first trouble which arose from his loose and vicious habits was an attempt made upon his life by Cleomenes, who found his palace in Alexandria had now become a prison. He took advantage of the king's being at Canopus, to escape from his guards, and to raise a riot in Alexandria; but not being able to gain the citadel, and seeing that disgrace and death must follow upon the failure of this mad undertaking, he stabbed himself with his own dagger.

Soon after this, Seleucia, the capital of Syria, which had been taken by Euergetes, was retaken by the young Antiochus, afterwards called the Great, or rather given up to him by the treachery of the garrison. Theodotus also, the Egyptian governor of Cœlo-Syria, offered to deliver up to him that province, and Antiochus marched southward, and had taken Tyre and Ptolemais before the Egyptian army could be brought into the field.

On this, Philopator for once roused himself from his idleness, and led the whole of his forces in person against the coming danger. He was followed by the royal guard of three thousand men under Eurylochus of Magnesia; two thousand peltastæ under Socrates of Bœotia; the phalanx of twenty-five thousand men under Andromachus and Ptolemy the son of Thaseas; eight thousand mercenaries under Phoxidas; the horse of the royal guard, the African horse, and the Egyptian horse, in all three thousand men, under Polycrates; the Greek and foreign horse, who were two thousand highly disciplined men, under Echecrates of Thessaly; three thousand Cretans under Cnopias of Alorus; three thousand Africans, armed like Macedonians, under Ammonius of Barce; the Egyptian phalanx of twenty thousand men under Sosibius, the king's chief adviser; and lastly, four thousand Gauls and Thracians under Dionysus of Thrace. There were in all seventy-three thousand men, and seventy-three elephants, or one elephant to every thousand men, which was the number usually allowed to the armies about this time.

With this army, followed by a fleet of transports, Philopator met Antiochus at Raphia, the border town between Egypt and Palestine. Arsinoë, his queen and sister, rode on horseback through the ranks, and called upon the soldiers to fight for their wives and children; and, though some of the Egyptian officers treacherously left their posts, and carried their troops over to Antiochus, yet the Syrian army was wholly routed, and Arsinoë enjoyed the knowledge and the praise of having been the chief cause of her husband's success.

Maccabees,
lib. iii.

By this victory Philopator regained Cœlo-Syria, and he then made a hasty and disgraceful treaty with the enemy, that he might the sooner get back to his life of ease.

Before going home he passed through Jerusalem, where he gave thanks, and sacrificed to God, in the Temple of the Jews; and, being struck with the beauty of the building, asked to be shown into the inner rooms. The priests told him of their law, by which every stranger, every Jew, and every priest but the high priest, was forbidden to enter the holy sanctuary; but Philopator roughly answered that he was not bound by the Jewish laws, and ordered them to lead him into the holy of holies.

The city was thrown into alarm by this unheard-of wickedness; the streets were filled with men and women in despair; the air was rent with shrieks and cries, and the priests prayed to Jehovah to guard his own temple from the stain. The king's mind, however, was not to be changed, the refusal of the priests only strengthened his wish, and all struggle was useless while the court of the Temple was filled with Greek soldiers. But the prayer of the priests was heard; the king, says the Jewish historian, fell to the ground in a fit, like a reed broken by the wind, and was carried out specchless by his friends and generals.

On his return to Alexandria he showed his hatred of the nation by his treatment of the Jews in his own kingdom. He made a law, that they should lose the rank of Macedonians, and be enrolled among the class of Egyptians. He ordered them to have their bodies marked with pricks, in the form of an ivy-leaf, in honour of Bacchus; and those who refused to have this done were outlawed, or forbidden to enter the courts of justice. This custom of marking the body, though not known among the Copts, must have been in use among the mixed race of Lower-Egyptians, Levit. xix. 28. even from the time of Moses, who forbad it in the Levitical law. It was used by the Arab prisoners of Rameses, and is still used by Lane's Egypt. the Egyptian Arabs of the present day.

The Egyptians, who, when the Persians were conquered by Alexander, could neither help nor hinder the Greek army, and who, when they formed part of the troops under the first Ptolemy, were uncounted and unvalued, had by this time been armed and disciplined like Greeks; and in the battle of Raphia the Egyptian Polybius, lib. v. phalanx had shown itself not an unworthy rival of the Macedonians. By this success in war, and by their hatred of their vicious and cruel king, the Egyptians were now for the first time encouraged to take arms against the Greek government. But history has told us nothing more of the rebellion, than that it was successfully put down; for, much as the Greeks were lowered in warlike courage by the wealth and luxury of Egypt, much as the Egyptians were raised by the Macedonian arms, the Greeks were still by far the better soldiers.

The ships built by Philopator do not raise his navy in our opinion, for they were more remarkable for their huge unwieldy size, their luxurious and costly furniture, than for their fitness for war.

Athenæus,
lib. v. 8.

One was four hundred and twenty feet long, and fifty-seven feet wide, with forty banks of oars. The longest oars were fifty-seven feet long, and weighted with lead at the handles, that they might be the more easily moved. This huge ship was to be rowed by four thousand rowers, its sails were to be shifted by four hundred sailors, and three thousand soldiers were to stand in ranks upon the deck. There were seven beaks in front, by which it was to strike and sink the ships of the enemy.

The royal barge, in which the king and court moved on the quiet waters of the Nile, was nearly as large as this ship of war. It was three hundred and thirty feet long, and forty-five feet wide; it was fitted up with state rooms and private rooms, and was nearly sixty feet high to the top of the royal awning.

lib. v. 10.

A third ship, which even surpassed these in its fittings and ornaments, was given to Philopator by Hiero king of Syracuse. It was built under the care of Archimedes, and its timbers would have made sixty triremes. Beside baths, and rooms for pleasures of all kinds, it had a library, and astronomical instruments, not for navigation, as in modern ships, but for study, as in an observatory. It was a ship of war, and had eight towers, from each of which stones were to be thrown at the enemy by six men. Its machines, like modern canons, could throw stones of three hundred pounds weight, and arrows of eighteen feet in length. It had four anchors of wood, and eight of iron. It was called the ship of Syracuse, but after it had been given to Philopator it was known by the name of the ship of Alexandria.

Livy,
lib. xxvii. 4.

During this reign the Romans were wholly taken up with their long and still doubtful war with Hannibal, and they sent ambassadors to renew their treaty of peace with Egypt. They sent as gifts robes of purple for Philopator and Arsinoë, and for Philopator a chair of ivory and gold, which was the usual gift of the republic to friendly kings. The Egyptians kept upon terms of friendship both with the Romans and the Carthaginians during the whole of the Punic wars.

When the city of Rhodes, which had long been joined in close friendship with Egypt, was shaken by an earthquake, that threw down the colossal statue of Apollo, together with a large part of the city walls and docks, Philopator was not behind the other friendly kings and states in his gifts and help. He sent to his brave allies a large sum of silver and copper, with corn, timber, and hemp.

Polybius, lib. v.

On the birth of his son and heir ambassadors crowded to Alexandria with gifts and messages of joy. But they were all thrown into the shade by Hircanus, the son of Joseph, who was sent from Jerusalem by his father, and who brought to the king one hundred boys and one hundred girls, each carrying a talent of silver.

Josephus, Antiq. xii. 4. B.C. 205.

Philopator, soon after the birth of this his only child, employed Philammon, at the bidding of his mistress, to put to death his queen and sister Arsinoë, or Eurydice, as she is sometimes called. He had already forgot his rank, and his name ennobled by the virtues of three generations, and had given up his days and nights to vice and riot. He kept in his pay several fools, or laughing-stocks as they were then called, who were the chosen companions of his meals; and was the first who brought eunuchs into the court of Alexandria.

Justinus, lib. xxx. 1.

Athenæus, lib. vi. 12.

His mistress Agathoclea, her brother Agathocles, and their mother Œnanthe, held the king bound by all those chains which clever, worthless, and selfish favourites throw around the mind of a weak and debauched king. Agathocles, who never left his side,

Justinus, lib. xxx. 1.

was his adviser in all matters of business or pleasure, and governed alike the army, the courts of justice, and the women. Thus was spent a reign of seventeen years, during which the king had never but once, when he met Antiochus in battle, roused himself from his life of sloth.

Polybius,
Excerpt. xv.
The misconduct and vices of Agathocles raised such an outcry against him, that Philopator, without giving up the pleasure of his favourite's company, was forced to take away from him the charge of receiving the taxes. That high post was then given to Tlepolemus, a young man, whose strength of body and warlike courage
Excerpt. xvi.
had made him the darling of the soldiers. Sosibius, also, was forced to give up to Tlepolemus the king's ring, or what in modern language would be called the great seal of the kingdom, the badge of office by which Egypt was governed; and the world soon saw that a body of luxurious mercenaries were as little able to choose a wise statesman as the king had been.

Excerpt. xv.
Sosibius had, indeed, made himself more hated than Agathocles; he had been the king's ready tool in all his murders. He had been stained, or at least reproached, with the murder of Arsinoë the daughter of Lysimachus, and Lysimachus the son of Philadelphus; then of Magas the son of Euergetes, and Berenice the widow of Euergetes; of Cleomenes the Spartan; and lastly, of Arsinoë the wife of Philopator.

But, with all his vices, Philopator had yet inherited the love of letters which has thrown so bright a light around the whole of the family; and to his other luxuries he sometimes added that of the society of the learned men of the Museum.

Diog. Laert.
When one of the professorships was empty, he wrote to Cleanthes, to ask him either to come to Alexandria himself, or to send him a philosopher whom he could recommend, and he sent Sphærus the

stoic, the pupil of Zeno. One day, when Sphærus was dining with the king, he said that a wise man should never guess, but only say what he knows. Philopator, wishing to tease him, ordered some waxen pomegranates to be handed to him, and, when Sphærus bit one of them, he laughed at him for guessing that it was a real fruit. But the stoic answered that there are many cases in which we must be guided by what seems probable.. None of the works of Sphærus have come down to us.

Eratosthenes, of whom we have before spoken, was librarian of the Museum during this reign; and Ptolemy, the son of Agesarchus, then wrote his history of Alexandria, a work now lost. Timæus also wrote his history of his own times, which Polybius made use of, and blamed for its mistakes.. Suidas.
Athenæus,
lib. x. 7.

Timæus, it seems, wrote his history in his own study, a thing which no modern historian would be afraid of being blamed for; but, when writing was little used, when letters between friends and public records were few, when there were no newspapers nor other helps to the historian, if he wished to get at the truth, he was forced to travel from place to place, to seek it upon the spot, or he would be often misled by hearsay. The division of labour was so little known in literature, that the historian ought to have been himself a traveller. Polybius,
lib. xii.

Philopator built a temple to Homer, in the middle of which he placed a sitting figure of the poet, and round it seven statues, meant for the seven cities which claimed the honour of giving him birth. He also built a small temple near Medinet Abu; his name is seen upon the temple of Karnak; and he added to the sculptures on the temple of Thoth at Pselcis in Ethiopia. Ælianus,
V. H. xiii. 22.

Wilkinson's
Thebes.

Some of his coins bear the words ΠΤΟΛΕΜΑΙΟΥ ΦΙΛΟΠΑΤΟΡΟΣ, 'of Ptolemy Philopator,' while those of the queen have ΑΡΣΙΝΟΗΣ Visconti,
Icon. Grec.

ΦΙΛΟΠΑΤΟΡΟΣ, ' of Arsinoë Philopator,' around the head. They are of a good style of art.

Josephus,
Antiq. xiii. 3.

Letronne,
Recherches.

The king was also sometimes named Eupator, and it was under that name that the people of Paphus set up a monument to him in the temple of Venus.

The first three Ptolemies had been loved by their subjects and feared by their enemies ; but Philopator, though his power was still acknowledged abroad, had by his vices and cruelty made himself hated at home, and had undermined the foundations of the government. He began his reign like an eastern despot ; instead of looking to his brother as a friend for help and strength, he distrusted him as a rival, and had him put to death. He employed the ministers of his vicious pleasures in the high offices of government ; and, instead of philosophers and men of learning, he brought

Porphyrius,
ap. Scal.

eunuchs into the palace as the companions of his son. He died, worn out with disease, in the seventeenth year of his reign, and about the forty-first of his age.

PTOLEMY EPIPHANES.

On the death of Philopator his son was only five years old. Agathocles, who had ruled over the country with unbounded power, endeavoured, by the help of Agathoclea and the other mistresses of the late king, to keep his death secret; so that, while the women seized the money and jewels of the palace, he might have time to take such steps as would secure his own power over the kingdom. But the secret could not be long kept, and Agathocles called together the citizens of Alexandria to tell them of the death of Philopator.

Justinus, lib. xxx. 2.
B.C. 204.

He went to the meeting, followed by his sister Agathoclea and the young Ptolemy, afterwards called Epiphanes. He began his speech, 'Ye men of Macedonia,' as this mixed body of Greeks, Jews, and Egyptians were always called. He wiped his eyes with his chlamys in well-feigned grief, and showed them their young king, who had been trusted, he said, by his father, to the care of Agathoclea and to their loyalty. He then accused Tlepolemus of aiming at the throne, and brought forward a creature of his own to prove the truth of the charge. But his voice was soon drowned in the loud murmurs of the citizens; they had smarted too long under his tyranny, and were too well acquainted with his falsehoods, to listen to any thing that he could say against his rival. Besides, Tlepolemus had the charge of supplying Alexandria with corn, a duty which was more likely to gain friends than the pandering to the vices of their hated tyrant. Agathocles soon

Polybius, lib. xv.

Poiybius,
lib. xv.

saw that his life was in danger, and he left the meeting in doubt whether he should seek for safety in flight, or boldly seize the power which he was craftily aiming at, and rid himself of his enemies by their murder.

While he was wasting these precious minutes in doubt, the streets were filled with groups of men, and of boys, who always formed a part of the mobs of Alexandria. They sullenly, but loudly, gave vent to their hatred of the minister, and if they had but found a leader they would have been in rebellion. In a little while the crowd moved off to the tents of the Macedonians, to learn their feelings on the matter, and then to the quarters of the mercenaries; and the mixed mob of armed and unarmed men soon told the fatal news, that the soldiers were as angry as the citizens. But they were still without a leader; they sent messengers to Tlepolemus, who was not in Alexandria, and he promised that he would soon be there; but perhaps he no more knew what to do than his guilty rival.

Agathocles, in his doubt, did nothing; he sat down to supper with his friends, perhaps hoping that the storm might blow over of itself, perhaps trusting to chance and to the strong walls of the palace. His mother Œnanthe ran to the temple of Ceres and Proserpine, and sat down before the altar in tears, believing that the sanctuary of the temple would be her best safeguard; as if the laws of God, which had never bound her, would bind her enemies. It was a festal day, and the women in the temple, who knew nothing of the storm which had risen in the forum within these few hours, came forward to comfort her; but she answered them with curses, she knew that she was hated, and would soon be despised, and she added the savage prayer, that they might have to eat their own children.

The riot did not lessen at sunset. Men, women, and boys were moving through the streets all night with torches. The crowds were greatest in the stadium and in the theatre of Bacchus, but most noisy in front of the palace. Agathocles was awakened by the noise, and in his fright ran to the bed-room of the young Ptolemy; and, distrusting the palace walls, hid himself, with his own family, the king, and two or three guards, in the underground passage which led from the palace to the theatre.

The night, however, passed off without any violence; but at day-break the murmurs became louder, and the thousands in the palace-yard called for the young king. By that time the Greek soldiers joined the mob, and then the guards within the gates were no longer to be feared. The gates were soon burst open, and the palace searched.

The mob rushed through the halls and lobbies, and learning where the king had fled, hastened to the underground passage. It was guarded by three doors of iron grating; but when the first was beaten in, Aristomenes was sent out to offer terms of surrender. Agathocles was willing to give up the young king, his misused power, his ill-gotten wealth and estates; he asked only for his life. But this was sternly refused, and a shout was raised to kill the messenger; and Aristomenes, the best of the ministers, whose only fault was the being a friend of Agathocles, and the having named his little daughter Agathoclea, would certainly have been killed upon the spot, if somebody had not reminded them that they wanted to send back an answer.

Agathocles, seeing that he could hold out no longer, then gave up the little king, who was set upon a horse, and led away to the stadium, amid the shouts of the crowd. There they seated him on the throne, and while he was crying at being surrounded by

Polybius,
lib. xv.

strange faces, the mob loudly called for revenge on the guilty ministers. Sosibius the somatophylax, the son of the former general of that name, seeing no other way of stopping the fury of the mob and the child's sobs, asked him if the enemies of his mother and of his throne should be given up to the people. The child of course answered ' yes,' without understanding what was meant, and on that they let Sosibius take him to his own house to be out of the uproar.

Agathocles was soon led out bound, and was stabbed by those who two days before would have felt honoured by a look from him. Agathoclea and her sister were then brought out, and lastly Œnanthe their mother was dragged away from the altar of Ceres and Proserpine. Some bit them, some struck them with sticks, some tore their eyes out ; as each fell down her body was torn to pieces, and her limbs scattered among the crowd—to such lengths of madness and angry cruelty was the Egyptian mob sometimes driven.

In the mean while some of the women called to mind that Philammon, who had been employed in the murder of Arsinoë, had within those three days come to Alexandria, and they made a rush at his house. The doors quickly gave way before their blows, and he was killed upon the spot by clubs and stones ; his little son was strangled by these raging mothers, and his wife dragged naked into the street, and there torn to pieces. Thus died Agathocles and all his family ; and the care of the young king then fell to Sosibius, the son of the late minister of that name, and to Aristomenes, who had already gained a high character for wisdom and firmness.

Justinus,
lib. xxxi. 1.

While Egypt was thus without a government, Philip of Macedonia and Antiochus of Syria agreed to divide the foreign provinces between them. Antiochus marched against Cœlo-Syria and Phenicia, and the guardians of the young Ptolemy sent against him an army under Scopas the Ætolian, who was at first successful, but was soon beaten by Antiochus, and driven back into Egypt. In these battles the Jews, who had not forgotten the ill-treatment that they had received from Philopator, joined Antiochus; and in return he released Jerusalem from all taxes for three years, and sent a large sum of money for the service of the Temple.

Josephus, Antiq. xii. 3.

Scopas, on his return to Egypt at the head of the mercenaries, formed a plot against the throne, and raised the city of Lycopolis, in the Busirite nome, in rebellion; but it was put down by Aristomenes and Polycrates, the latter of whom had commanded the cavalry at the battle of Raphia, and had since been governor of Cyprus. Scopas and the other ringleaders were put to death.

Polybius, lib. xvii. Rosetta Stone.

About this time the Romans sent ambassadors to Alexandria, to tell the king that they had conquered Hannibal, and to thank him for the friendship of the Egyptians during that long and doubtful war, when so many of their nearer neighbours had joined the enemy. They begged that if the senate felt called upon to undertake a war against Philip, who, though no friend to the Egyptians, had not yet taken arms against them, it might cause no breach in the friendship between the king of Egypt and the Romans.

Livy, lib. xxxi. 2. B.C. 201.

This was almost the last time that the Greek kingdom of Egypt was treated with the respect which the wisdom and courage of the first Ptolemies had gained for it. The vices and follies of Philopator had undermined a throne which, though raised with great skill, rested upon a weak foundation.

There was not in Alexandria, what indeed is rarely to be found anywhere, virtue enough in the people to give strength and firmness to the government when the character of the sovereign failed. Nor was there in the place of it a body of men, who, having through their wealth and birth a stake in the country worth guarding, and a hold on the minds of their countrymen, take care, for their own sakes, both to uphold the throne and to check its too great power.

Perhaps there was not much virtue among the philosophers and men of letters, who were the chief men of Alexandria. But, even if there had been, virtue and talent, among a people who were themselves without virtue, would not have stood in the place of high birth. The men of letters were employed as ambassadors, and as ministers of the crown, but they had no weight of their own. The form of government was an unmixed monarchy; and though the last king had made his power felt through his wide provinces, the government was almost overthrown because his son chanced to be a minor.

Justinus, lib. xxx. 2.

In answer to this embassy, the Alexandrians sent to Rome a message, which was meant to place the kingdom wholly in the hands of the senate. It was to beg them to undertake the guardianship of the young Ptolemy, and the defence of the kingdom against Philip and Antiochus during his childhood.

The Romans, in return, gave the wished-for answer; they sent ambassadors to Antiochus and Philip, to order them to make no attack upon Egypt, on pain of falling under the displeasure of the senate; and they sent Marcus Lepidus to Alexandria, to govern the foreign affairs of the kingdom, under the modest name of tutor to the young king.

Goltzius, de re Numm.

This high honour was afterwards mentioned by Lepidus, with pride, upon the coins struck when he was consul, in the eighteenth year of this reign. They have the city of Alexandria on the one side, and on the other the words TUTOR REGIS, among other titles, with the figure of the Roman in his toga, putting the diadem on the head of the young Ptolemy. But the coins struck by Sextus Ælius Catus, when he was ædile in the eighth year of this reign, and was employed to bring corn from Africa for the use of Rome, seem to claim for the Roman people sovereign power over Egypt, as on one side of them is the very eagle and thunderbolt which we see on almost all the coins of the Ptolemies.

Livy,
lib. xxxi. 50.

The haughty orders of the senate at first had very little weight with the two kings. Antiochus conquered Phenicia and Cœlo-Syria; and he was then met by a second message from the senate, who no longer spoke in the name of their ward, the young king of Egypt, but ordered him to give up to the Roman people the states which he had seized. On this, Antiochus made peace with Egypt by a treaty, in which he betrothed his daughter Cleopatra to the young Ptolemy, and added the disputed provinces of Phenicia and Cœlo-Syria as a dower, which were to be given up to Egypt when the king was old enough to be married.

Justinus,
lib. xxxi. 1.

Hieronymus,
in Dan. xi.
B.C. 198.

Philip marched against Athens, and the other states of Greece which had heretofore held themselves independent and in alliance with Egypt; and when the Athenians sent to Alexandria to beg for the usual help, the Egyptians felt themselves so much in the power of the senate, that they sent to Rome to ask whether they should help their old friends the Athenians against Philip, the common enemy, or whether they should leave it to the Romans to help them. And these haughty republicans, who wished all their allies to forget the use of arms, who valued their friends not for their strength but for their obedience, sent them word that the senate did not wish them to help the Athenians, and that the Roman people would take care of their own allies.

Livy,
lib. xxxi. 9.

If we now look back for two centuries, to the time when Egypt fought its battles and guarded its coasts by the help of Greek arms, and remark that from that time it sunk till it became a province of Macedonia, we cannot fail to see that the Greek kingdom of Egypt was in its turn at this time falling by the same steps by which it had then risen, and that it was already, though not in name yet in reality, a Roman province. But while, during this second fall, the Egyptians looked upon the proud but unlettered Romans only as friends, as allies, who asked no tribute, who took no pay, who fought only for ambition and for the glory of their own country, we cannot but remark, and with sorrow for the cause of arts and letters, that in their former fall the Egyptians had only seen the elegant and learned Greeks in the light of mean hirelings, of mercenaries who fought with equal pleasure on either side, and who looked only for their pay, with very little thought about the justice of the cause, or their country's greatness. While we thus look at the two nations, we are strongly reminded of the virtues which the Romans gained with their strict feelings of clanship or pride of country, and which the Greeks, after the time of Alexander, lost by becoming philosophic citizens of the world.

Polybius, lib. xvii. B. C. 197.

Soon after this, the battle of Cynocephalæ in Thessaly was fought between Philip and the Romans, in which the Romans lost only seven hundred men, while as many as eight thousand Macedonians were left dead upon the field. This battle, though only between Rome and Macedonia, must not be passed unnoticed in the history of Egypt, where the troops were armed and disciplined like Macedonians; as it was the first time that the world had seen the Macedonian phalanx routed and in flight before any troops not so armed.

The phalanx was a body of spearsmen, in such close array that each man filled a space of only one square yard. The spear was seven yards long, and, when held in both hands, its point was five yards in front of the soldier's breast. There were sixteen ranks of these men, and when the first five ranks lowered their spears the point of the fifth spear was one yard in front of the foremost rank. The Romans, on the other hand, fought in open ranks, with one yard between each, or each man filled a space of four square yards, and in a charge would have to meet ten Macedonian spears.

But then the Roman soldiers went into battle with very different feelings from the Greeks. In Rome, arms were trusted only to citizens, who had a country to love, a home to guard, and who had some share in making the laws which they were called upon to obey. But the Greek armies of Macedonia, Egypt, and Syria were made up either of natives who bowed their necks in slavery, or of mercenaries who made war their trade, and rioted in its lawlessness; both of whom felt that they had little to gain from victory, and nothing to lose by a change of masters.

Moreover, the warlike skill of the Romans was far greater than any that had yet been brought against the Greeks. They saw that the phalanx could use its whole strength only on a plain; that a wood, a bog, a hill, or a river were difficulties which this close body of men could not always overcome. A charge or a retreat equally lessened its force; the phalanx was meant to stand the charge of others. The Romans, therefore, chose their own time and their own ground, they loosened their ranks and widened their front, avoided the charge, and attacked the Greeks at the side and in the rear; and the fatal discovery was at last made, that the Macedonian phalanx was not unconquerable. This news must have been heard by every statesman of Egypt and the East with

Polybius,
lib. xvii.

alarm; the Romans were now their equals, or even their masters, and we can hardly believe that the prophecy of Lycophron, that 'the children of Æneas would hold the sceptre of the sea and land,' could have been written before this battle was fought.

But to return to Egypt; Polycrates, beside having been of use in crushing the rebellion of Scopas, and in holding the island of Cyprus faithfully for the king during these times of trouble, had likewise made himself of weight, by bringing over with him from Cyprus the taxes of that island, which were much wanted in the empty treasury. He now advised that they should declare the minority at an end, and that the king was of age: for though Ptolemy was only fifteen years old, and had not reached the age which the law had fixed, yet Polycrates thought that it might add some strength to his weak government, or at least get rid of the Roman guardianship; and accordingly, in the ninth year of his reign, the young king was crowned with great pomp at Memphis, the ancient capital of the kingdom.

B.C. 196.

Rosetta Stone.

On this occasion he came to Memphis, by barge, in grand state, where he was met by the priests of Upper and Lower Egypt, and crowned in the temple of Pthah with the double crown called Pschent, the crown of the two provinces. After the ceremony the priests made the Decree in honour of the king, which is carved on the stone known by the name of the Rosetta Stone, in the British Museum.

Ptolemy is there styled ' King of Upper and Lower Egypt, son of the gods Philopatores, approved by Pthah, to whom Ra has given victory, a living image of Amun, son of Ra, Ptolemy immortal, beloved by Pthah, god Epiphanes most gracious.' In the date of the decree we are told the names of the priests of Alexander, of the gods Soteres, of the gods Adelphi, of the gods Euergetæ, of the gods Philopatores, of the god Epiphanes himself, of Berenice Euergetis, of Arsinoë Philadelphus, and of Arsinoë Philopator. The preamble mentions with gratitude the services of the king, or rather of his wise minister Aristomenes; and the enactment orders that the statue of the king shall be worshipped in every temple of Egypt, and be carried out in the processions with those of the gods of the country; and lastly, that the decree is to be carved at the foot of every statue of the king, in sacred, in common, and in Greek writing.

It is to this stone, with its three kinds of writing, and to the skill and industry of Dr. Young, that we now owe our knowledge of hieroglyphics. The Greeks of Alexandria, and after them the Romans, who might have learned how to read this kind of writing if they had wished, seem never to have taken the trouble; it fell into disuse on the rise of Christianity in Egypt; and it was left for an Englishman to unravel the hidden meaning after it had been forgotten for nearly fifteen centuries. *Young's Hierog. Disc.*

During the minority of the king the taxes were lessened; the crown debtors were forgiven; those who were found in prison charged with crimes against the state were released; the allowance from government for upholding the splendour of the temples was continued, as was the rent from the glebe or land belonging to the priests; the first fruits, or rather the taxes paid by the priests to the king on the year of his coming to the throne, which we may suppose were by custom allowed to be less than what the law ordered, were not increased; the priests were relieved from the heavy burthen of making a yearly voyage to do homage at Alexandria; there was a stop put to the pressing of men for the navy, which had been felt as a great cruelty by an inland people whose habits and religion alike made them hate the sea, and this *Rosetta Stone.*

was a boon which was the more easily granted, as the navy of
Alexandria, which was built in foreign dockyards and steered by
foreign pilots, had very much fallen off in the reign of Philopator.
The duties on linen cloth, which was the chief manufacture of the
kingdom, and, after corn, the chief article exported, were lessened;
the priests, who manufactured linen for the king's own use, probably for the cloathing of the army, and the sails for the navy,
were not called upon for so large a part of what they made as before; and the royalties on the other linen manufactories, and the
duties on the samples or patterns, both of which seem to have been
unpaid for the whole of the eight years of the minority, were wisely
forgiven.   All the temples of Egypt, and that of Apis at Memphis
in particular, were enriched by his gifts; in which pious works,
in grateful remembrance of their former benefactor, and with a
marked slight towards Philopator, they said that he was following
the wishes of his grandfather the god Euergetes.

From this decree we gain some little insight into the means by
which the Ptolemies raised their taxes, and we also learn that they
were so new and foreign from the habits of the people that they
had no Egyptian word by which they could speak of them; and
therefore borrowed the Greek word *Syn-taxes*, as we have since
done.

Early Hist.
plate 6.

History gives us many examples of kings who like Epiphanes
gained great praise for the weakness and mildness of the government, during their minorities. Aristomenes the minister, who had
governed Egypt for Epiphanes, fully deserved that trust. While
the young king looked up to him as a father, the country was
well governed and his orders obeyed; but as he grew older his
good feelings were weakened by the pleasures which usually beset
youth and royalty. The companions of his vices gained that power

Diod. Sic.
Excerpt. 294.

over his mind which Aristomenes lost, and it was not long before Excerpt. 297. this wise tutor and counsellor was put to death by being ordered to drink poison. Epiphanes then lost that love of his people which the wisdom of the minister had gained for him; and he governed the kingdom with the cruelty of a tyrant, rather than with the legal power of a king. Even Aristonicus his favourite eunuch, who Polybius, Excerpt. xxi. was of the same age as himself, and had been brought up as his play-fellow, passed him in the manly virtues of his age, and earned the praise of the country for setting him a good example, and checking him in his career of vice.

In the thirteenth year of his reign, when he reached the age of Hieronymus, in Dan. xi. B.C. 192. eighteen, Antiochus the Great sent his daughter Cleopatra into Egypt, and the marriage, which had been agreed upon six years before, was then carried into effect; and the provinces of Cœlo-Syria and Phenicia, which had been promised as a dower, were, in form at least, handed over to the generals of Epiphanes.

Cleopatra was a woman of strong mind and enlarged understanding; and Antiochus hoped, that, by means of the power which she would have over the weak mind of Epiphanes, he should gain more than he lost by giving up Cœlo-Syria and Phenicia. But she acted the part of a wife and a queen, and instead of betraying her husband into the hands of her father, she was throughout the reign his wisest and best counsellor.

The war was still going on between Antiochus and the Romans, Livy, lib. xxxvi. 4. B.C. 191. and Epiphanes soon sent to Rome a thousand pounds weight of gold and twenty thousand pounds of silver, to help the republic against their common enemy; but the Romans neither hired mercenaries nor fought as such, the thirst for gold had not yet become the strongest feeling in the senate, and they sent back the money to Alexandria with many thanks.

Rosetta Stone. At the beginning of this reign a rebellion had broken out at Lycopolis, in the Delta, which ended by that city being besieged and taken by the king's troops; and in the latter years of the reign, Polybius, Excerpt. xx. unless the historian has fallen into a mistake in the name of the city, Lycopolis was again the seat of civil war. At the head of the rebellion were Athinis, Posiris, Chesuphis, and Irobashtus, whose Coptic names clearly prove that it was a struggle on the part of the Egyptians to throw off the Greek yoke. But they could not long hold out against Polycrates at the head of the Greek mercenaries, and, yielding to the greater force of the besiegers, and to the king's promises of pardon, they came out of their stronghold, and were brought to the king at Sais.

Epiphanes, in whose heart were joined the cruelty and the cowardice of a tyrant, who had not even shown himself to the army during the siege, was now eager to act the conqueror; and in spite of the promises of safety on which these brave Copts had laid down their arms, he had them tied to his chariot wheels, and, copying the vices of men whose virtues he could not even understand, like Achilles and Alexander, he dragged them living round the city walls, and then ordered them to be put to death.

Suidas. Apollonius, whom we have spoken of in the reign of Euergetes, and who had been teaching at Rhodes during the reign of Philopator, was recalled to Alexandria in the beginning of this reign, and made librarian of the Museum.

Visconti, Icon. Grec. The coins of this king are known by the glory or rays of sun which surround his head, and which agrees with his name Epiphanes, '*illustrious*,' or as it is written in the hieroglyphics 'light-bearing.' On the other side is the cornucopia between two stars, with the words ΒΑΣΙΛΕΩΣ ΠΤΟΛΕΜΑΙΟΥ, '*of King Ptolemy*.'

No temples, and few additions to temples, seem to have been

built in Upper Egypt during this reign, which began and ended in
rebellion. We find however a Greek inscription at Philæ, of ' King Hieroglyphics, plate 65.
Ptolemy and queen Cleopatra, gods Epiphanes, and of Ptolemy
their son, to Asclepius,' a god whom the Egyptians called Imothph
the son of Pthah.

Cyprus and Cyrene were nearly all that were left to Egypt of
its foreign provinces. The cities of Greece, which had of their own
wish put themselves under Egypt for help against their nearer
neighbours, now looked to Rome for that help; the greater part
of Asia Minor was under Antiochus the Great; Cœlo-Syria and
Phenicia, which had been given up to Epiphanes, had been again
soon lost; and the Jews, who in all former wars had sided with the
kings of Egypt, as being not only the stronger but the milder rulers,
now joined Antiochus. The ease with which the wide-spreading
provinces of this once mighty empire fell off, almost without a
shake, from the decayed trunk, showed how the whole had been
upheld by the wisdom and warlike skill of its kings, rather than
by a deep-rooted hold in the habits of the people. The trunk indeed was never strong enough for its branches; and, instead of
wondering that the handful of Greeks in Alexandria, on whom
the power rested, lost those wide provinces, we should rather wonder that they were ever able to hold them.

But Epiphanes planned an attack upon Cœlo-Syria, against the Hieronymus, in Dan. xi.
advice of his generals. He is said to have been asked by one of
them, how he should be able to pay for the large forces which he
was getting together for that purpose; and he playfully answered,
that his treasure was in the number of his friends. But his joke
was taken in earnest; they were afraid of new taxes and fresh levies
on their estates, and means were easily taken to poison him. He Porphyrius, ap. Scalig.
died in the twenty-ninth year of his age, after a reign of twenty-

four years; leaving the navy unmanned, the army in disobedience, the treasury empty, and the whole frame-work of government out of order.

Polybius, Legat. lvii.
Just before his death he had sent to the Achaians to offer to send ten gallies to join their fleet; and Polybius the historian, to whom we owe so much of our knowledge of these reigns, although he had not yet reached the age called for by the Greek law, was sent by the Achaians as one of the ambassadors, with his father, to return thanks; but before they had quitted their own country they were stopt by the news of the death of Epiphanes.

Those who took away the life of the king seem to have had no thoughts of mending the form of government, nor any plan by which they might lessen the power of his successor. It was only one of those outbreaks of private vengeance which have often happened in unmixed monarchies, where men are taught that the only way to check the king's tyranny is by his murder; and the little notice that was taken of it by the people proves their want of public virtue as well as of political wisdom.

PTOLEMY PHILOMETOR.

Porphyrius,
ap. Scalig.
B.C. 180.

EPIPHANES left behind him two sons, each named Ptolemy, and a daughter named Cleopatra; the elder son, though still a child, mounted the throne under the able guardianship of his mother Cleopatra, and took the very suitable name of Philometor, or *mother-loving*.

Polybius,
Legat. 78.
B.C. 173.

When Philometor reached his fourteenth year, the age at which his minority ceased, the Anacleteria, or ceremony of his coronation, was celebrated with great pomp. Ambassadors from several foreign states were sent to Egypt to wish the king joy, to do honour to the day, and to renew the treaties of peace with him: Caius Valerius and four others were sent from Rome; Apollonius, the son of Mnestheus, was sent from Judæa; and we may regret with Polybius that he himself was not able to form part of the embassy then sent from the Achaians, that he might have been able to see the ceremony and give us an account of it.

Livy,
lib. xlii. 6.
2 Maccabees,
iv. 21.

While Cleopatra lived, she had been able to keep her son at peace with her brother Antiochus Epiphanes, and to guide the vessel of the state with a steady hand. But upon her death Leneus and the eunuch Eulaius, who then had the care of the young king, sought to reconquer Cœlo-Syria; and they embroiled the country in a war at a time when weakness and decay might have been seen in every part of the army and navy, and when there was the greatest need of peace. Cœlo-Syria and Phenicia had been given to Ptolemy Epiphanes as his wife's dower; but, when Philometor seemed too

Hieronymus,
in Dan. xi.

Polybius,
Legat. 82.
weak to grasp them, Antiochus denied that there had ever been such a treaty, and got ready to march against Egypt, as the easiest way to guard Cœlo-Syria.

Hieronymus,
in Dan. xi.
When Antiochus entered Egypt he was met at Pelusium by the army of Philometor, which he at once routed in a pitched battle. The whole of Egypt was then in his power; he marched upon Memphis with a small force, and seized it without having to strike a blow, helped perhaps by the plea that he was acting on behalf of his nephew Ptolemy Philometor, who then fell into his hands.

Porphyrius,
ap. Scalig.
B.C. 170.
On this, the younger Ptolemy, the brother of Philometor, who was with his sister Cleopatra in Alexandria, and was about fifteen Livy,
lib. xliv. 19. years old, declared himself king, and sent ambassadors to Rome to ask for help against Antiochus; and, taking the name of the most popular of his forefathers, he called himself Euergetes II. He is however better known in history as Ptolemy Physcon, or *bloated,* a nickname which was afterwards given to him when he had grown fat and unwieldy from disease and luxury.

Antiochus threw a bridge across the Nile and sat down before Alexandria. The Egyptians could not show themselves in the field against the larger army of Syria, and if he could have carried the lib. xlv. 11. city by storm he would have been master of all Egypt. But the ambassadors of Rome, who, on hearing of this inroad of the Syrians, had lost no time on their journey, then landed at Alexandria, and, though they brought no force with them to add weight to their commands, they ordered Antiochus and both the brothers to cease from war immediately, on pain of their displeasure. This threat was enough; Antiochus withdrew his army, and left Euergetes king of the Greeks at Alexandria, and Philometor king of the rest of Egypt, except Pelusium, where he himself left a strong garrison that he might easily re-enter Egypt whenever he chose.

Ptolemy Macron, the Egyptian governor of Cyprus, added to the troubles of the country by giving up his island to Antiochus. But he met with the usual fate of traitors, he was badly rewarded; and when he complained of his treatment, he was called a traitor by the very men who had gained by his treachery, and he poisoned himself in the bitterness of his grief. Little as we know of his name, the historian can still point to it to prove the folly of wickedness. 2 Maccabees, x. 13.

Antiochus, like most invaders, carried off whatever treasure fell into his hands. Egypt was a sponge which had not lately been squeezed, and his court and even his own dinner-table then shone with a blaze of silver and gold unknown in Syria before this inroad into Egypt. Athenæus, lib. v. 5.

By these acts, and by the garrison left in Pelusium, the eyes of Philometor were opened, and he saw that his uncle had not entered Egypt for his sake, but to make it a province of Syria, after it had been weakened by civil war. He therefore wisely forgave his rebellious brother and sister in Alexandria, and sent offers of peace to them; and it was agreed that the two Ptolemies should reign together, and turn their forces against the common enemy. It was most likely at this time, and as a part of this treaty, that Philometor married his sister Cleopatra; a marriage which, however much it may shock our feelings of right, was not forbidden either by the law or custom of the country. Livy, lib. xlv. 11.

On this treaty between the brothers the year was called the twelfth of Ptolemy Philometor and the first of Ptolemy Euergetes, and the public deeds of the kingdom were so dated. Porphyrius, ap. Scalig. B.C. 170.

The next year Antiochus Epiphanes again entered Egypt, and Memphis opened its gates to him without a battle. He came down towards Alexandria, and crossed the Nile at Leucine, four miles from the city gates. There he was again met by the Roman Livy, lib. xlv. 12.

ambassadors, who ordered him to quit the country. On his hesi-
tating, Popilius, who was one of them, drew a circle round him on
the sand with his stick, and told him that, if he crossed that line
without promising to leave Egypt at once, it should be taken as a
Livy,
lib. xlv. 13.
declaration of war against Rome. On this threat Antiochus again
quitted Egypt, and the brothers sent ambassadors to Rome to
thank the senate for their help, and to acknowledge that they
owed more to the Roman people than they did to the gods or to
their forefathers.

lib. xlvi. 21.
The unhappy quarrels between the brothers, however, soon
broke out again, and, as the party of Euergetes was the stronger,
Philometor was driven from his kingdom, and he fled to Rome for
safety and for help. He entered the city privately, and took up
his lodgings in the house of one of his own subjects, a painter of
Alexandria. His pride led him to refuse the offers of better enter-
tainment which were made to him by Demetrius, the son of Seleucus, who like himself was hoping to regain his kingdom by the
help of the Romans. The kings of Egypt and Syria, the two
greatest kingdoms in the world, were at the same time asking to
be heard at the bar of the Roman senate, and were claiming the
thrones of their fathers at the hands of men who could make and
unmake kings at their pleasure.

As soon as the senate heard that Philometor was in Rome, they
lodged him at the cost of the state in a manner becoming his high
lib. xlvi. 22.
rank, and soon sent him back to Egypt, with orders that Euergetes
should reign in Cyrene, and that the rest of the kingdom should
Porphyrius,
ap. Scalig.
belong to Philometor. This happened in the seventeenth year of
B. C. 164.
Philometor and the sixth of Euergetes, which was the last year that
was named after the two kings.

Cassius Longinus, who was next year consul at Rome, and Juventius Thalna, who was consul the year after, were, most likely, Goltzius, de re Numm. among the ambassadors who replaced Philometor on the throne; for they both of them put the Ptolemaic eagle and thunderbolt on their coins, as though to claim the sovereignty of Egypt for the senate.

To these orders Euergetes was forced to yield; but the next Livy, lib. xlvi. 32. Polybius, Legat. 113. year he went himself to Rome to complain to the senate that they had made a very unfair division of the kingdom, and to beg that they would add the island of Cyprus to his share. After hearing the ambassadors of Philometor, the senate granted the prayer of Euergetes, and sent ambassadors to Cyprus, who had orders to hand that island over to Euergetes, and to make use of the fleets and armies of the republic, if these orders were disobeyed.

During his stay in Rome, Euergetes, if we may believe Plutarch, Plutarch. Gracchus. made an offer of marriage to Cornelia, the mother of the Gracchi; but the offer of a throne could not make that high-minded matron quit her children and her country.

He left Rome with the Roman ambassadors, and in passing Polybius, Legat. 115. through Greece he raised a large body of mercenaries to help him to wrest Cyprus from his brother, as it would seem that the governor, faithful to his charge, would not listen to the commands of Rome. But the ambassadors had been told to conquer Cyprus, if necessary, with the arms of the republic only, and they therefore made Euergetes disband his levies. They sailed for Alexandria to enforce their orders upon Philometor, and sent Euergetes home to Cyrene.

Philometor received the Roman ambassadors with all due honours; he sometimes gave them fair promises, and sometimes put them off till another day; and tried to spin out the time without saying either yes or no to the message of the senate. Euergetes sent to Alexandria to ask if they had gained their point; but though they threatened to return to Rome if they were not at once obeyed, Philometor, by his kind treatment and still kinder words, kept them more than forty days longer at Alexandria.

Polybius, Legat. 116.

At last the Roman ambassadors left Egypt, and on their way home they went to Cyrene, to let Euergetes know that his brother had disobeyed the orders of the senate; and Euergetes sent two ambassadors to Rome to beg them to revenge their affronted dignity and to enforce their orders by arms. The senate of course declared the peace with Egypt at an end, and ordered the ambassadors of Philometor to quit Rome within five days, and sent ambassadors to Cyrene to tell Euergetes of their decree.

Legat. 115.

But, while this was going on, the state of Cyrene had risen in arms against Euergetes; his vices and cruelty had made him hated, they had gained for him the nicknames of Kakergetes, or *mischief-maker*, and Physcon, or *bloated*; and while wishing to gain Cyprus

Legat. 132.

he was in danger of losing his own kingdom. When he marched against the rebels he was beaten and wounded, either in the battle, or by an attack upon his life afterwards.

When he had at last put down this rising he sailed for Rome to urge his complaints against Philometor, upon whom he laid the blame of the late rebellion; and the senate, after hearing both sides, sent a small fleet with Euergetes, not large enough to put him on the throne of Cyprus, but gave their allies in Greece and Asia leave to enlist as mercenaries under his standard.

Excerpt. 31.

The Roman troops seem not to have helped Euergetes, but he landed in Cyprus with his own mercenaries, and was there met by Philometor who had brought over the Egyptian army in person: Euergetes was soon forced to shut himself up in the city of Lapitho, and at last to lay down his arms before his elder brother.

If Philometor had upon this put his brother to death, the deed would have seemed almost blameless after the family murders at which we have already shuddered in this history. But, with a goodness of heart which is rarely met with in the history of kings, and which, if we looked up to merit as much as we do to success, would throw the warlike virtues of his forefathers into the shade, he a second time forgave his brother all that had passed, he replaced him on the throne of Cyrene, and promised to give him his daughter in marriage.

We are not told whether the success in arms and forgiving mildness of Philometor had turned the Roman senate in his favour, or whether their troops were wanted in other quarters; but at any rate they left off trying to enforce their decree; Philometor kept Cyprus, and sent Euergetes a yearly gift of corn from Alexandria.

Diodorus Sic. Excerpt. 334.

At a time when so few great events cross the stage we must not let the fall of Macedonia pass unnoticed. We have seen the conquests in Europe, Asia, and Africa, by Macedonian valour under Alexander the Great, and on his death the Egyptian and other great kingdoms founded by his generals. We have since seen the Macedonian phalanx routed at Cynocephalæ; and lastly, in this reign, Macedonia was conquered by the Romans, the king led in triumph to Rome, and, in the insulting decree of the senate, the people declared free. But the Macedonians had never learnt to govern themselves. The feelings which in a commonwealth would be pride of country, in a monarchy are entwined round the throne, as in an army round the standard, and when these are lost they are not easily regained. At any rate we never again meet with Macedonia on the page of history.

During the wars in Syria between Philometor and Antiochus

Josephus,
Bell. Jud. i. 1.
Antiq. xiii. 6.
Epiphanes, at the beginning of this reign, the Jews were divided
into two parties, one favouring the Egyptians and one the Syrians.
At last the Syrian party drove their enemies out of Jerusalem, and
Onias the high priest, with a large body of Jews, fled to Egypt.
There they were well received by Philometor, who gave them leave
to dwell in the neighbourhood of Heliopolis, perhaps on the very
spot which had been given to their forefathers when they entered
Egypt under Jacob.

Onias built his temple at Leontopolis near Bubastus, on the site
of an old Egyptian temple, which had fallen into disuse and decay.
It was built after the model of the temple of Jerusalem, and though
Hieronymus,
in Dan. xi.
by the Jewish law there was to be no second temple, yet Onias
defended himself by quoting the words of Isaiah, who foretold that
Chap. xix. 19.
' in that day there should be an altar to the Lord in the midst of
the land of Egypt.'

Josephus,
in Apion. ii.
Onias was much esteemed by Philometor, and bore high offices
in the government; as also did Dositheus, another Jew, who had
been very useful in helping the king to crush a rebellion.

Inscript.
Letronne,
Recherches.
Since the Ptolemies had found themselves too weak to hold
Ethiopia, they had placed a body of soldiers on the border of the
two countries, to guard Egypt from the inroads of the enemy.
This camp at Parembole had by degrees grown into a city, and, as
most of the soldiers were Greek mercenaries, it was natural that
the temple which Philometor built there should be dedicated in
the Greek language. Of the temples hitherto built by the Ptolemies, every one seems to have had the king's name and titles, and
its dedication to the gods, carved on its massive portico in hieroglyphics; but this was dedicated to Isis and Serapis, on behalf of
Philometor and his queen, in a Greek inscription.

Philometor also built a temple at Antæopolis, to Antæus, a god of whom we know nothing, but that he gave his name to the city, and another to Aroëris at Ombos; and in the same way he carved the dedications on the porticoes in the Greek language. This custom became common after that time, and proves both the lessened weight which the native Egyptians bore in the state, and that the kings had forgotten the wise rules of Ptolemy Soter, in regard to the religious feelings of the people. They must have been greatly shocked by this use of foreign writing in the place of the old characters of the country, which, from having been used in the temples, even for ages beyond the reach of history, had at last been called sacred.

It is to this reign, also, that we seem to owe the great temple at Apollinopolis Magna, although it was not finished till one or two reigns later. It is one of the largest and least ruined of the temples of Egypt. Its chief parts are the flat-roofed body of the temple; the lofty portico, with a front of six columns, which being taller than the former part seems like a building by itself; then the courtyard in front of the portico, with columns and a roof round the walls; and lastly the two huge square towers, with sloping sides, and between them is the narrow doorway into the court-yard, which is the only opening in its massive walls. As a castle it must have had great strength, and as it was in the hands of the Egyptians, is the strongest proof that they were not distrusted by their Greek rulers. *Wilkinson's Thebes.* *Denon, pl. 58.*

The old religion of the country was perhaps in the Delta falling into disuse, some of the Egyptian temples below Memphis were in ruins; while the Greek language had become so common that even in the last reign it was called 'Lower Egyptian writing'; and even in Thebes the legal deeds were sometimes written in duplicate, in Egyptian and Greek. *Josephus, Antiq. xiii. 6.* *Vocab.Hierog. p. 110. Papyrus, Young's Disc.*

Some light may be thrown upon the priesthood in this reign by one of these deeds; which is a sale by the priests of one half of a third of their collections for the dead who had been buried in Thynabunum, the Libyan suburb of Thebes. This sixth share of the collections consisted of seven or eight families of slaves; the price of it was four hundred pieces of brass; the bargain was made in the presence of sixteen witnesses, whose names are given; and the deed was registered and signed by one of the public officers of the city of Thebes.

This custom of giving offerings to the priests for the good of the dead would seem to have been a cause of some wealth to the temples, and must have been common even in the time of Moses. It was one among the many Egyptian customs forbidden by that lawgiver, and most likely continued in use at least from his time till the time of this deed.

Aristarchus, who had been the tutor of Euergetes II., and of a son of Philometor, was one of the ornaments of this reign. He had been a pupil of Aristophanes the grammarian, and had then studied under Crates at Pergamus. He died at Cyprus, whither he probably withdrew himself on the death of Philometor. He was chiefly known for his critical writings, in which his opinions of poetry were thought so just that few dared to disagree with them, and his name soon became proverbial for a critic.

Aristarchus had also the good fortune to be listened to in his lecture-room by one whose name is far more known than those of his two royal pupils. Moschus of Syracuse, the pastoral poet, was one of his hearers; but his fame must not be claimed for Alexandria, he can hardly have learned from the critic that just taste by which he joined softness and sweetness to the rude plainness of the Doric muse. Indeed in this he only followed his young friend Bion,

Deuteron. xxvi. 14.

Suidas.

whose death he so beautifully bewails, and from whose poems he generously owns that he learned so much. It may be as well to add, that the lines in which he says that Theocritus, who had been dead a century, joined with him in his sorrow for the death of Bion are later additions not found in the early manuscripts of his poems.

It has sometimes been made a question how far the poet and orator have been helped forward, or even guided, by the rules of the critic ; and at other times it has been thought that the more tender flowers of literature have rather been choked by this weed which entwined itself round them. But history seems to teach us that neither of these opinions is true. While Aristarchus was writing there were no poets in Alexandria to be bound down by his laws, no orators to be tamed by the fear of his lashes : and, on the other hand, none wrote at his bidding or rose to any real height by the narrow steps by which he meant them to climb. It would seem as if the fires of genius and of liberty had burned out together, as if the vices which were already tainting the manners had also poisoned the literary taste of the Alexandrians. The golden age of poetry had passed before the brazen age of criticism began. The critics wrote at a time when the schools of literature would have been still more barren without them.

Nicander the poet and physician is also claimed by Alexandria, [Tzetzes in Lycophronte.] though part of his renown was shed upon Pergamus, where he lived under king Attalus. He has left a poem in quaint and learned phrase, on poisons, and the poisonous bites and stings of animals, and on their remedies. Thus, in the place of poetry, we now only meet with science put into verse. [Suidas.]

But by far the greatest man of Alexandria at this time was Hipparchus, the father of mathematical astronomy. Aristillus and [Ptolemy, lib. iii. iv. vi.]

Timocharis had before made a few observations on the fixed stars, but Hipparchus was the first to form a catalogue of any size. His great observations were made with a fixed armillary sphere, or rather a fixed instrument having a plane parallel to the equator, and gnomon parallel to the earth's pole. If he was the inventor of this instrument, it was at least made upon principles known to Eratosthenes, and contained in his Theory of Shadows.

With this instrument he noted the hour of the equinoctial day on which the sun shone equally upon the top and the bottom of the equatorial plane; that hour was the time of the equinox. By making many such observations he learned the length of the year, which he found was less than three hundred and sixty-five days and a quarter. He found that the four quarters of the year were not of equal length. He also made the great discovery of the precession of the equinox, or that the sidereal year, which is measured by the stars, was not of the same length as the common year, which is measured by the seasons. Thus he found that the star *Spica Virginis*, which in the time of Timocharis had been eight degrees before the equinoctial point, was then only six degrees before it. Hence he said that the precession of the equinox was not less than one degree in a century, and added, that it was not along the equator but along the ecliptic. He was a man of great industry, and unwearied in his search after truth; and he left a name that was not equalled by that of any astronomer in the fifteen centuries which followed.

Hero, the pupil of Ctesibius, ranked very high as a mathematician and mechanic. He has left a work which treats upon several branches of mechanics: on making warlike machines for throwing stones and arrows; and on automatons, or figures which were made to move, as if alive, by machinery under the floor. His chief work is on pneumatics, on making forcing pumps and fountains by the force of the air. Among other clever toys he made birds which sang, or at least uttered one note, by the air being driven by water out of a close vessel through small pipes. Other playthings were moved by the force of air rarified by heat; and one, to which the modern discovery of the steam-engine has given a value which it by no means deserved, was moved by the force of steam. The steam was driven into a vessel through a hole in the axis on which it was to turn, and rushed out of it through two holes in the line of its tangents; so that the vessel turned round on the well-known prin- Ferguson's
Lectures. ciple of Barker's mill.

The portrait of the king is known from those coins which bear Visconti,
Icon. Grec. the words ΒΑΣΙΛΕΩΣ, ΠΤΟΛΕΜΑΙΟΥ ΘΕΟΥ ΦΙΛΟΜΗΤΟΡΟΣ, '*of King Ptolemy the mother-loving god.*' The eagle on the other side of the coin has a phœnix or palm branch on his wing or by his side. We have not before met with the title ΘΕΟΥ, '*god,*' on the coins of the Ptolemies, but as every one of them had been so called in the hieroglyphical inscriptions, it can scarcely be called new.

The palm-branch or phœnix is the hieroglyphical character for Vocab. Hier.
No. 636, 645. ' year,' and it seems to have been placed upon the coins in acknow- ledgement of the return of quiet and good government during the latter half of this reign, after two reigns of misrule and trouble; but as the reasons for this conjecture are rather far fetched it will be best to explain them. The civil year had only three hundred and sixty-five days, and hence the new-year's day, which ought to have fallen, with the rising of Sirius and the overflow of the Nile, in the middle of July, came one day earlier every four years. It had been in its right place in the year B.C. 1321; and it would again be right, after four times three hundred and sixty-five years, in the year A.D. 140. This second coming of the Phœnix, as it was called, was looked for as the return of the golden age. It was however a long time to wait for, and the Egyptians fancied that each quarter of the time had been marked by the reign of a king of more than usual greatness. These kings were Sesostris, Amasis, and Euergetes, who, if Sesostris be meant for Shishank, reigned about three hundred and sixty-five years after one another, and after the year B. C. 1321. But in this reign, as at the end of that of Tiberius, the Egyptians, without waiting for the year A. D. 140, seem to have thought that the phœnix had returned to the land with all the blessings of good government.

Tacitus,
Annal. iv.

Polybius,
Excerpt. 31.

When Philometor quitted the island of Cyprus after beating his brother in battle, he left Archias as governor, who entered into a plot to give it up to Demetrius king of Syria for the sum of five hundred talents. But his plot was found out, and he then put an end to his own life, to escape from punishment and self-reproach.

Justinus,
lib. xxxv. 1.

1 Maccabees,
ch. x.

By this treachery of Demetrius, Philometor was made his enemy, and he joined Attalus king of Pergamus and Ariarathes king of Cappadocia in setting up Alexander Balas as a pretender to the throne of Syria, who beat Demetrius in battle, and put him to death. Philometor than gave his elder daughter Cleopatra in marriage to Alexander, and led her himself to Ptolemais, where the marriage was celebrated with great pomp.

Josephus,
Antiq. xiii. 8.

But even in Ptolemais, the city in which Alexander had been so covered with favours, Philometor was near falling under the treachery of his new son-in-law. He learned that a plot had been formed against his life by Ammonius, and he wrote to Alexander to beg that the traitor might be given up to justice. But Alexander acknowledged the plot as his own, and refused to give up his servant. On this, Philometor recalled his daughter, and turned against Alexander the forces which he had led into Syria to uphold him. He then sent to the young Demetrius, the son of his late enemy, to offer him the throne and wife which he had lately given to Alexander Balas, and Demetrius was equally pleased with the two offers. Philometor then entered Antioch at the head of his army, and, after being crowned king of Asia and Egypt, with a forbearance then very uncommon, he called together the council of the people and persuaded them to receive Demetrius as their king.

Philometor and Demetrius then marched against Alexander, routed his army, and drove him into Arabia. But in this battle Philometor's horse was frightened by the braying of an elephant, and threw the king into the ranks of the enemy, and he was taken up covered with wounds. He lay speechless for five days, and the surgeons then endeavoured to cut out a piece of the broken bone from his skull. He died under the operation; but not before the head of Alexander had been brought to him as the proof of his victory.

Livy, Epit. lii.

Josephus, Antiq. xiii. 8.

Thus fell Ptolemy Philometor, the last of the Ptolemies to whom history can point with pleasure. His reign began in trouble: before he had reached the years of manhood the country had been overrun by foreigners, and torn to pieces by civil war; but he left the kingdom stronger than he found it, a praise which he alone can share with Ptolemy Soter. He was alike brave and mild; he was the only one of the race who fell in battle, and the only one whose hands were unstained with civil blood. At an age and in a country when poison and the dagger were too often the means by which the king's authority was upheld, when goodness was little valued, and when conquests were thought the only measure of greatness, he had spared the life of a brother taken in battle, he had refused the crown of Syria when offered to him; and not only

Polybius, Excerpt. 31.

no one of his friends or kinsmen, but no citizen of Alexandria, had
been put to death during the whole of his reign. We find grateful inscriptions to his honour at the city of Citium in Cyprus, in
the island of Theræ, and at Methone in Argolis.

Inscript.
Letronne,
Recherches.

Philometor had reigned thirty-five years; eleven years alone,
partly while under age, then six years jointly with his brother
Euergetes II., and eighteen more alone while his brother reigned
in Cyrene. He had married his sister Cleopatra, and left her a
widow, with two daughters each named Cleopatra, and a son named
Ptolemy. The elder daughter we have seen offered to Euergetes,
then married to Alexander Balas, and lastly to Demetrius. The
younger daughter, afterwards known by the name of Cleopatra
Cocce, and the son, were still in the care of their mother. He had
most likely had another son, who had been the pupil of Aristarchus, and who had died before his father; as the little elegy which
is addressed to the dying child on the grief of his father and mother, by Antipator of Sidon, would seem to be meant for a son of
Philometor.

Porphyrius,
ap. Scalig.

Anthologia
Græca.

PTOLEMY EUERGETES II.

On the death of Philometor, his widow Cleopatra and some of the chief men of Alexandria proclaimed his young son king, most likely under the name of Ptolemy Eupator; but Euergetes, whose claim was favoured by the mob, marched from Cyrene to Alexandria to seize the crown of Egypt. Onias the Jew defended the city for Cleopatra; but a peace was soon made by the help of Thermus the Roman ambassador, by which it was agreed that Euergetes should be king, and marry Cleopatra, his sister and his brother's widow. We may take it for granted that one article of the treaty was that her son should reign on the death of his uncle, but Euergetes, forgetting that he owed his own life to Philometor, had the boy put to death on the day of the marriage.

The Alexandrians, after the vices and murders of former kings, could not have been much struck by the behaviour of Euergetes towards his family; but he was not less cruel towards his people. Alexandria, which he had entered peaceably, was handed over to the unbridled cruelty of the mercenaries, and blood flowed in every street. The population of the city, which was made up of Jews and Greeks of all nations, who looked upon it less as a home than as a place of trade in which they could follow their callings with the greatest gain, quitted Alexandria as easily as they had come there under Ptolemy Soter; and Euergetes, who was afraid that he should soon be left to reign over a wilderness, made new laws in favour of trade and of strangers who would settle there.

Justinus,
lib. xxxviii. 8.
B.C. 145.

Letronne,
Recherches.

Josephus,
in Apion. ii.

Justinus,
lib. xxxviii. 8.

Porphyrius, ap. Scalig.

In the lifetime of Philometor he had never laid aside his claim to the throne of Egypt, but had only yielded to the commands of Rome and to his brother's forces, and he now numbered the years of his reign from his former seizing of Alexandria. He had reigned six years with his brother, and then eighteen years in Cyrene, and he therefore called the first year of his reign the twenty-fifth.

Diodorus Sic. Excerpt. 354.

In the next year he went to Memphis to be crowned; and, while the pomps and rites were there being performed, his queen and sister bore him a son, whom he named from the place, and to please the people, Memphites. But his queen was already in disgrace; and some of those very friends who on his brother's death had marched with him against Alexandria were publicly put to death for speaking ill of his mistress Eirene.

Justinus, lib. xxxviii. 8.

He soon afterwards put away his wife and married her younger daughter, his niece Cleopatra Cocce; and for this and other acts against his family and his people he lived hated by every body.

Athenæus, lib. xii. 12.

He was so bloated with disease that his body was nearly six feet round, and he was made weak and slothful by this weight of flesh. He never walked without a crutch, and he wore a loose robe like a woman's, which reached to his feet and hands. On the year that he was chosen priest of Apollo by the Cyrenæans, he showed his pleasure at the empty honour by feasting in a most costly manner all those who had before filled that office.

Justinus, lib. xxxviii. 8.

Such was the man who received Scipio Africanus the younger and the other Roman ambassadors who were sent by the senate to see that the kingdom of their ally was peaceably settled. Euergetes went to meet him with great pomp, and received him with all the honours due to his rank, and the whole city followed him in crowds through the streets, eager to catch a sight of the con-

queror of Carthage, of the greatest man who had been seen in
Alexandria, of one who had by his virtues and his triumphs added
a new glory even to the name of Scipio.

Euergetes showed him over the palace, and the treasury; but, Diod. Sic.
Legat. 32.
though the Romans had already begun to run the down-hill race
of luxury, in which the Egyptians were so far ahead of them, yet
Scipio, who held to the old fashions and plain manners of the republic, was not dazzled by mere gold and purple. But the trade
of Alexandria, the natural harbour, the forests of masts, and the
lighthouse, the only one in the world, passed any thing that his well-
stored mind had looked for.

He went by boat to Memphis, and saw the rich crops on either
bank, and the easy navigation of the Nile, in which the boats were
sailing up the river by the force of the wind and floating down by
the force of the stream. The villages on the river side were large
and thickly set, and the crowded population was well fed and well
clothed. The Roman statesman saw that nothing was wanting
but a good government to make Egypt what it used to be, the
greatest kingdom in the world.

Scipio went no higher than Memphis; the buildings of Upper
Egypt, the oldest and the largest in the world, could not draw
him to Thebes, a city whose trade had fallen off, where the depo-
sits of bullion in the temples had lessened, and whose linen manufacture had moved towards the Delta. Had this great statesman
been a Greek he would perhaps have gone on to this city, famous
alike in history and in poetry; but as it was, Scipio and his friends
then sailed for Cyprus, Syria, and the other provinces or kingdoms under the power of Rome, to finish this tour of inspection.

The kind treatment shown to these and other Romans is also Inscript.
Letronne,
Recherches.
proved by an inscription set up in the island of Delos by Lucius

and Caius Pedius, in gratitude to this king. It is on a monument dedicated to Apollo and Artemis; but they have not told us whether they were visitors, or whether they were employed in the service of Euergetes.

1 Maccabees,
xiv. xv.
B.C. 143.

For some time past the Jews, taking advantage of the weakness of Egypt and Syria, had been struggling to make themselves free; and, at the beginning of this reign, Simon Maccabæus the high priest sent an embassy to Rome, with a shield of gold weighing one thousand minæ, as a present, to get their independence acknowledged by the Romans. On this the senate made a treaty of alliance with the family of the Maccabees, and, using the high tone of command to which they had for some time past been accustomed, they wrote letters to Euergetes and the king of Syria ordering them not to make war upon their friends the Jews.

Diod. Sic.
Excerpt. 361.

The vices and cruelty of Euergetes called for more than usual skill in the minister to keep down the angry feelings of the people. This skill was found in the general Hierax, who was one of those men whose popular manners, habits of business, and knowledge of war make them rise over every difficulty in times of trouble. On him rested the whole weight of the government; his wise measures in part made up for the vices of his master, and, when the treasure of the state had been turned to the king's pleasures, and the soldiers were murmuring for want of pay, Hierax brought forward his own money to quiet the rebellion.

Livy,
Epit. 59.

But at last the people could bear their grievances no longer, the soldiers without pay, instead of guarding the throne, were its greatest enemies, and the mob rose in Alexandria, set fire to the palace, and Euergetes was forced to leave the city and withdraw to Cyprus.

The Alexandrians, when free from their tyrant, sent for Cleopatra his sister and divorced queen, and set her upon the throne. Her son by Philometor, in whose name she had before claimed the throne, had been put to death by Euergetes; her son by Euergetes was with his father in the island of Cyprus; and this cruel monster, fearing that Cleopatra might make use of his son's name to strengthen her throne, had the child put to death.

The birthday of Cleopatra was at hand, and it was to be cele- Diod. Sic.
Excerpt. 374. brated in Alexandria with the usual pomp; and Euergetes, putting the head, hands, and feet of his son Memphites into a box, sent it to Alexandria by a messenger, who had orders to deliver it to Cleopatra in the midst of the feast, when the nobles and ambassadors were making their accustomed gifts.

The grief of Cleopatra was only equalled by the anger of the Alexandrians, who the more readily armed themselves under Marsyas and marched against the army of Euergetes under Hegelochus. But the Egyptian army was beaten on the Syrian frontier, and Marsyas sent prisoner to Euergetes; who then showed the only act of mercy which can be mentioned to his praise, and spared the life of a prisoner whom he thought he could make use of.

Cleopatra then sent to Syria, to her son-in-law Demetrius, to Justinus,
lib. xxxix. 1. ask for help, which was at first readily granted, but Demetrius was soon called home again by a rising in Antioch.

Great indeed must be the cruelty which a people will not bear from their own king rather than call in a foreign master to relieve them. Among the various feelings by which men are governed, few are stronger than the wish for national independence; hence the return of the hated and revengeful Euergetes was not dreaded so much by the Alexandrians as the being made a province of Syria. Cleopatra received no help from Demetrius, but she lost the love of her people by asking for it, and she was soon forced to fly from Alexandria. She put her treasures on board a ship and joined

Inscript.
Letronne,
Recherches.

Demetrius in Syria, while Euergetes regained his throne. It would seem, however, that she was again allowed to return to Egypt, as we find her name joined with those of Euergetes and his queen in one of the public acts of the priests.

Though the discontent of the people did not again show itself in rebellion, it still broke out in loud murmurs, and a petition of the priests of Isis, begging to be relieved from the unlawful and ruinous demands which were made upon them by the officers of the crown, proves the nature of the misgovernment.

The trade of the Egyptians had given them very little knowledge of geography beyond their own coasts. Indeed the whole trade of the ancients was carried on by buying goods from their nearest neighbours on one side, and selling them to those on the other side of them. Long voyages were wholly unknown; and though the trading wealth of Egypt had mainly risen from carrying the merchandize of India and Arabia Felix from the ports on the Red Sea to the ports on the Mediterranean, the Egyptians seem to have gained no knowledge of the countries from which these goods came. They bought them of the Arab traders, who came to Cosseir and Berenice from the opposite coast; the Arabs had probably bought them from the caravans that had carried them across the desert from the Persian gulf; and, that these land-journies across the desert were both easier and cheaper than a coasting voyage, we have before learned, from Philadelphus thinking it worth while to build watering and resting-houses in the desert between Coptos and Berenice, to save the coasting voyage of about equal length, between Berenice and Cosseir.

India seems to have been only known to the Greeks as a country that by sea was to be reached by the way of the Euphrates and the Persian Gulf; and though Scylax had, by the orders of Darius, dropt down the River Indus, coasted Arabia, and thence reached the Red Sea, this voyage was either forgotten or disbelieved, and in the time of the Ptolemies it seems probable that nobody thought that India could be reached by sea from Egypt. Arrian indeed thought that the difficulty of carrying water in their small ships, with large crews of rowers, was alone great enough to stop a voyage of such a length along a desert coast that could not supply them with fresh water. *Nearchus, Periplus.*

The long voyages of Solomon and Necho had been limited to coasting Africa; the voyage of Alexander the Great had been from the Indus to the Persian Gulf; hence it was that the court of Euer- *Strabo, lib. ii.* getes was startled by the strange news that the Arabian guards on the coast of the Red Sea had found a man in a boat by himself, who could not speak Coptic, but whom they afterwards found was an Indian, who had sailed straight from India, and had lost his shipmates. He was willing to show any one the route by which he had sailed; and Eudoxus Cyzicenus came to Alexandria to try to persuade Euergetes to give him the command of a vessel for this voyage of discovery. A vessel was given him; and though he was but badly fitted out he reached India by sea, and brought back a cargo of spices and precious stones. After the death of Euergetes he was again sent on the Indian voyage by Cleopatra, and, being better fitted out, his voyage was more successful. He wrote an account of the coasts which he visited, and it was made use of by Pliny.

But the art of navigation was so far unknown that but little use was made of this discovery; the goods of India, which were all costly and of small weight, were still for the most part carried across the desert on camels' backs, and we may remark that hardly more than twenty small vessels ever went to India in one year during the reigns of the Ptolemies, and that it was not till Egypt was a province of Rome that the trade-winds across the Arabian Sea were found out by Hippalus, a pilot in the Indian trade. The voyage was little known in the time of Pliny; and Palmyra and Petra, the two chief cities in the desert, whose whole wealth rested and whose very being hung upon their being watering places for these caravans, were still wealthy cities in the second century of our era, when the voyage by the Arabian Sea became for the first time easier and cheaper than the journies across the desert.

Euergetes had been a pupil of Aristobulus, a learned Jew, a writer of the peripatetic sect of philosophers, and also of Aristarchus the grammarian; and though he had given himself up to the lowest pleasures, yet he held with his crown that love of letters and learning which had ennobled his forefathers. He was himself an author, and like Ptolemy Soter wrote his Memorabilia, or an account of what he had seen most remarkable in his lifetime. We may suppose that his writings were not of a very high order; they were quoted by Athenæus who wrote in the reign of Marcus Aurelius; but we learn little else from them than the names of the mistresses of Ptolemy Philadelphus, and that a flock of pheasants was kept in the palace of Alexandria. He also wrote a commentary on Homer, of which we know nothing.

In this reign the schools of Alexandria, though not holding the rank which they had gained under Philadelphus, were still highly thought of. The king still gave public salaries to the professors, and Panaretus, who had been a pupil of the philosopher Arcesilaus, received the very large sum of twelve talents, or two thousand pounds a-year.

Sositheus, and his rival the younger Homer, the tragic poets of this reign, have even been called two of the Pleiades of Alexan-

Pliny, lib. vi.

2 Maccabees, i. 10.
Clem. Alex. Strom. i.
Athenæus, lib. ii. 84.

lib. xiii. 5.
lib. xiv. 20.
lib. ii. 58.

Suidas.

dria; but that was a title given to many authors of very different ages, and to some of very little merit.

But, unfortunately, the larger number of the men of letters had in the late wars taken part with Philometor against the cruel and luxurious Euergetes. Hence, when the streets of Alexandria were flowing with the blood of those whom he called his enemies, crowds of learned men left Egypt, and were driven to earn a livelihood by teaching in the cities to which they then fled. The isles and coasts of the Mediterranean were so filled with grammarians, philosophers, geometers, musicians, schoolmasters, painters, and physicians, that the cruelty of Euergetes II., like the taking of Constantinople by the Turks, may be said to have spread learning by the ill-treatment of its professors.

Athenæus, lib. iv. 29.

The city which was then rising highest in arts and letters was Pergamus in Asia Minor, which under Eumenes and Attalus was almost taking the place which Alexandria had before held. Its library already held two hundred thousand volumes, and raised a jealousy in the mind of Euergetes. Not content with buying books and adding to the size of his own library, he wished to lessen the libraries of his rivals; and, nettled at the number of volumes which Eumenes had got together at Pergamus, he made a law forbidding the export of the Egyptian papyrus on which they were written. On this the copiers employed by Eumenes wrote their books upon sheepskins, which were called *charta pergamena,* or parchment, from the name of the city in which they were written. Thus our own two words, parchment from *Pergamus,* and paper from *papyrus,* remain as monuments of the rivalry in book-collecting between the two kings.

Pliny, lib. xiii. 21.

But even money and the commands of kings could not procure faultless copies of the books wanted; and Galen, who lived in Per-

Galen, in Hippocrat. ii. de Nat. Hom.

gemus under the Antonines, complains woefully of the treatment which authors had received from these hasty copiers.

Porphyrius, ap. Scalig.

Euergetes had reigned six years with his brother, then eighteen years in Cyrene, and lastly twenty-nine years after the death of his brother, and he died in the fifty-fourth year of his reign. He left a widow, Cleopatra Cocce ; two sons, Ptolemy and Ptolemy Alexander ; and three daughters, Cleopatra, married to her elder brother, Tryphæna, married to Antiochus Gryphus, and Selene unmarried ; and also a natural son, Ptolemy Apion, to whom by will he left the

Justinus, lib. xxxix. 3.

kingdom of Cyrene, while he left the kingdom of Egypt to his widow and one of his sons, giving her the power of choosing which should be her colleague.

CLEOPATRA COCCE, AND PTOLEMY SOTER II.

ON the death of Euergetes, his widow Cleopatra Cocce would Justinus,
lib. xxxix. 3.
B.C. 116. have chosen her younger son Ptolemy Alexander, then a child, for her partner on the throne, most likely because it would have been longer in the course of years before he would have claimed his share of power; but she was forced by a threatened rising of the Alexandrians to make her elder son king. Before, however, she would do this, she made a treaty with him, which would strongly prove, if any thing were still wanting, the vice and meanness of the Egyptian court. It was, that, although married to his sister Cleopatra, of whom he was very fond, he should put her away and marry his younger sister Selene; because the mother hoped that Selene would be false to her husband's cause, and weaken his party in the state by her treachery: she planned the unhappiness of two children and the guilt of a third. Perhaps history can hardly show another marriage so wicked and unnatural, or a reign so little likely to end without a civil war. The mother and the son were jointly styled sovereigns of Egypt; but they lived apart, and in distrust of one another, each surrounded by his own friends; while Cleopatra's stronger mind and greater skill in king-craft gained for her the larger share of power. Can we wonder that under such heads the monarchy was tottering to its fall?

Ptolemy took the name of Soter II., though he is more often called Lathyrus from a wart or stain upon his face; he was also Pausanias,
lib. i. 9. called Philometor; and we learn from an inscription on a temple

Inscript.
Letronne,
Recherches.

at Apollinopolis Parva, that both these names formed part of the style in which the public acts ran in this reign; it is dedicated by ' the queen Cleopatra and king Ptolemy, gods Philometores, Soteres, and his children,' without mentioning his wife. The name of Philometor was given to him by his mother, because, though he had reached the years of manhood, she wished to act as his guardian; but her unkindness to him was so remarkable that historians have thought that it was a nickname.

Justinus,
lib. xxxix. 3.

Cleopatra the daughter, who gained our pity for being put away by her husband at the command of her mother, soon forfeited it by the steps which she then took. She made a treaty of marriage with Antiochus Cyzicenus, the friend of her late husband, who was struggling in unnatural warfare for the throne of Syria with his brother Antiochus Grypus, the husband of her sister Tryphæna; and in her way to Syria she stopped at Cyprus, where she raised a large army, and took it with her as her dower, to help her new husband against his brother and her sister.

With this army Cyzicenus met his brother in battle, and was beaten; and Cleopatra shut herself up in the city of Antioch. Grypus and Tryphæna then laid siege to the city, and Tryphæna soon took her revenge on her sister for coming into Syria to marry the brother and rival of her husband. The city was taken, and Tryphæna ordered her sister to be torn from the temple into which she had fled, and to be put to death. In vain Grypus urged that he did not wish his victory to be stained with the death of a sister; that Cleopatra was by marriage his sister as well as hers; that she was the aunt of their children; and that the gods would punish them if they dragged her from the altar. But Tryphæna was merciless and unmoved; she gave her own orders to the soldiers, and Cleopatra was killed clinging with her arms to the statue of the goddess.

This unnatural cruelty however was soon overtaken by punishment: in the next battle Cyzicenus was the conqueror, and he put Tryphæna to death, to quiet the ghost of her murdered sister.

In the third year of her reign Cleopatra Cocce gave the island of Cyprus to her younger son Alexander, as an independant kingdom, thinking that he would be of more use to her there, in upholding her power against his brother Lathyrus, than he could be at Alexandria.

Porphyrius, ap. Scalig. B.C. 113. Pausanias, lib. i. 9.

She had given the command of her army to two Jews, Chelcias, and Ananias the son of Onias the priest of Heliopolis; and hence, when the war broke out between the Jews and Samaritans, Cleopatra helped the Jews, and perhaps for that same reason Lathyrus helped the Samaritans. He sent six thousand men to his friend Antiochus Cyzicenus to be led against the Jews, but this force was beaten by the two sons of Hyrcanus the high priest.

Josephus, Antiq. xiii. 18.

By this act Lathyrus must have lost the good will of the Jews of Lower Egypt, who, since their countrymen had raised Judæa to the rank of a free state, found themselves of great weight in Alexandria and in the Egyptian army. Hence Cleopatra again ventured to choose her own partner on the throne. She raised a riot in Alexandria against him, in the tenth year of their reign, on his putting to death some of her friends, or more likely, as Pausanias says, by showing to the people some of her eunuchs covered with blood, who she said were wounded by him; and she forced him to fly from Egypt. She took from him his wife Selene, whom she had before thrust upon him, and who had borne him two children; and allowed him to withdraw to the kingdom of Cyprus, from which she recalled her favourite son Alexander to reign with her in Egypt.

Porphyrius, ap. Scalig.

Justinus, lib. xxxix. 4.

During these years the building was going forward of the beautiful temple at the city afterwards named by the Romans Contra-

Wilkinson's Thebes.

Denon, pl. 53. Latopolis, on the other side of the Nile from Latopolis or Esne. Little now remains of it but its massive portico, upheld by two rows of four columns each, having the sun with outstretched wings carved on the overhanging eaves. The earliest names found among the hieroglyphics with which its walls are covered are those of Cleopatra Cocce and her son Ptolemy Soter, while the latest name is that of the emperor Commodus. Even under Cleopatra Cocce, who was nearly the worst of the family, the building of these great temples did not cease.

CLEOPATRA COCCE, AND PTOLEMY ALEXANDER.

THE two sons were so far puppets in the hands of their clever but wicked mother, that on the recalling of Alexander no change was seen in the government beyond that of the names which were placed at the head of the public acts. The former year was called the tenth of Cleopatra and Ptolemy Soter, and this year was called the eleventh of Cleopatra and eighth of Ptolemy Alexander; as Alexander counted his years from the time when he was sent with the title of king to Cyprus.

B. c. 106.

Porphyrius, ap. Scalig.

While the kingdoms of Egypt and Syria were alike weakened by civil wars and by the vices of their kings, Judæa, as we have seen, had risen under the wise government of the Maccabees to the rank of an independant state; and latterly, Aristobulus the eldest son of Hircanus, and afterwards Alexander Jannæus his second son, had made themselves kings. But Gaza, Ptolemais, and some other cities bravely refused to part with their liberty, and sent to Lathyrus, then king of Cyprus, for help. This was not however done without many misgivings; for some were wise enough to see that, if Lathyrus helped them, Cleopatra would on the other hand help their king Jannæus; and when Lathyrus landed at Sicaminos with thirty thousand men, the citizens of Ptolemais refused even to listen to a message from him.

Josephus, Antiq. xiii. 20.

The city of Gaza then eagerly sent for the help which Ptolemais refused. Lathyrus drove back Jannæus, and marched upon Asochis a city of Galilee, where he scaled the walls on the sabbath-day, and

Josephus,
Antiq. xiii. 21.
took ten thousand prisoners and a large booty. He then sat down before the city of Sapphoris, but left it on hearing that Jannæus was marching against him on the other side of the Jordan, at the head of a force larger than his own. He crossed the river in face of the Jewish army and routed it with great slaughter. The Jewish historian adds that between thirty and fifty thousand men were slain upon the field of battle, and that the women and children of the neighbouring villages were cruelly put to death.

Cleopatra now began to fear that her son Lathyrus would soon make himself too powerful if not checked in his career of success, and that he might be able to march upon Egypt. She therefore mustered her forces and put them under the command of Chelcias and Ananias, her Jewish generals. She sent her treasure, her will, and the children of Alexander, to the island of Cos, as a place of safety, and then marched with the army into Palestine, having sent forward her son Alexander with the fleet. By this movement Lathyrus was unable to keep his ground in Cœlo-Syria, and he took the bold step of marching towards Egypt. But he was quickly followed by Chelcias, and his army was routed though Chelcias lost his life in the battle.

Cleopatra, after taking Ptolemais, sent part of her army to help that which had been led by Chelcias; and Lathyrus was forced to shut himself up in Gaza. Soon after this the campaign ended, by Lathyrus returning to his own kingdom of Cyprus, and Cleopatra to Egypt.

On this success, Cleopatra was advised to seize upon the throne of Jannæus, and again to add to Egypt the provinces of Palestine and Cœlo-Syria, which had so long made part of the kingdom of her forefathers. We may be quite sure that this cruel overbearing woman, who had never yet been guided by any feeling of right or dislike for war, did not yield to the reasons of her general Ananias through any kind feeling towards his countrymen: but the Jews of Lower Egypt were too strong to be treated with slight; it was by the help of the Jews that Cleopatra had driven her son Lathyrus out of Egypt; they formed a large part of the Egyptian armies, which were no longer even commanded by Greeks; and it must have been by these clear and unanswerable reasons that Ananias was able to turn the queen from the thoughts of this conquest, and to renew the league between Egypt and Judæa.

Cleopatra however was still afraid that Lathyrus would be helped by his friend Antiochus Cyzicenus to conquer Egypt, and she therefore kept up the quarrel between the brothers by again sending troops to help Antiochus Grypus; and lastly, she sent him in marriage her daughter Selene, whom she had before forced upon Lathyrus.

Justinus,
lib. xxxix. 4.

Ptolemy Alexander, who had been a mere tool in the hands of his mother, was at last tired of his gilded chains: but he saw no means of throwing them off, and of gaining that power in the state which his birth and title, and the age which he had then reached, ought to have given him. The army was in favour of his mother, and an unsuccessful effort would certainly have been punished with death; so he took perhaps the only path open to him, he left Egypt by stealth, and chose rather to quit his throne and palace than to live surrounded by the creatures of his mother and in daily fear for his life.

Cleopatra might well doubt whether she could keep her throne against both her sons, and she therefore sent messengers with fair promises to Alexander, to ask him to return to Egypt. But he knew his mother too well ever again to trust himself in her hands; and while she was taking steps to have him put to death on his return, he formed a plot against her life by letters. In this double game Alexander had the advantage of his mother; her character was so well known that he needed not to be told of what was going on; while she perhaps thought that the son whom she had so long ruled as a child would not dare to act as a man. Alexander's plot was of the two the best laid, and on his reaching Egypt his mother was put to death.

Porphyrius, ap. Scalig.

Thus died by the orders of her favourite son, after a reign of twenty-eight years, this wicked woman, who had married the husband of her mother, who had made her daughters marry and leave their husbands at her pleasure, who had made war upon one son and had plotted the death of the other.

Justinus, lib. xxxix. 5.

But Alexander did not long enjoy the fruits of his murder. The next year the Alexandrians rose against him in a fury. He was hated not perhaps so much for the murder of his mother as for the cruelties which he had been guilty of, or at least had to bear

Porphyrius, ap. Scalig.

the blame of, while he reigned with her. His own soldiers turned against him, and he was forced to seek his safety by flying on board a vessel in the harbour, and he left Egypt with his wife and daughter.

He was followed by a fleet under the command of Tyrrhus, but he reached Myræ, a city of Lycia, in safety: and afterwards, in crossing over to Cyprus, he was met by an Egyptian fleet under

B.C. 87.

Chæreas and killed in battle.

Though others may have been guilty of more crimes, Alexander had perhaps the fewest good qualities of any of the family of the Lagidæ. During his idle reign of twenty years, in which the crimes

Athenæus, lib. xii. 12.

ought in fairness to be chiefly laid to his mother, he was wholly given up to the lowest and worst of pleasures, by which his mind and body were alike ruined. He was so bloated with vice and disease, that he seldom walked without crutches; but at his feasts he could leap from his raised couch and dance with naked feet upon the floor with the companions of his vices. He was blinded by flattery, ruined by debauchery, and hated by the people.

His coins are not easily known from those of the other kings, which also bore the words ΠΤΟΛΕΜΑΙΟΥ ΒΑΣΙΛΕΩΣ, '*of Ptolemy the king*,' round the eagle; but one, on which are rams-horns to the head, is no doubt of this king, as the ram's-horns were symbolical of Alexander the Great, whose name he bore.

Numismata Pembroch.

Some of the coins of his mother have the same words round the eagle on one side, while on the other is her head, with a helmet formed like the head of an elephant, or her head with the words ΒΑΣΙΛΙΣΣΗΣ ΚΛΕΟΠΑΤΡΑΣ, '*of Queen Cleopatra*.' There are other coins with the same head of Cleopatra, with two eagles to point out the joint sovereignty of herself and her son.

Visconti, Icon. Grec.

British Museum.

History has not told us who was the first wife of Alexander, but he left a son by her named after himself Ptolemy Alexander, who we have seen sent by his grandmother for safety to the island of Cos, the fortress of the family, and a daughter whom he carried with him in his flight to Lycia. His second wife was Cleopatra Berenice, the daughter of his brother Lathyrus, by whom he had no children, and who is called in the hieroglyphics his queen and sister.

Porphyrius, ap. Scalig.

Wilkinson's Thebes.

In the middle of this reign died Ptolemy Apion the king of Cyrene. He was the half brother of Lathyrus and Alexander, and having been made king of Cyrene by his father Euergetes II. he had reigned there quietly for twenty years. Being between Egypt and Carthage, then called the Roman province of Africa, and having no army which he could lead against the Roman legions, he had placed himself under the guardianship of Rome; he had

Livy, Epit. lxx. B. c. 97.

bought a truce during his lifetime, by making the Roman people his heirs in his will.

Cyrene had been part of Egypt for above two hundred years, and was usually governed by a younger son or brother of the king. But on the death of Ptolemy Apion, the Roman senate, who had latterly been grasping at everything within their reach, claimed his kingdom as their inheritance, and in the flattering language of their decree by which the country was enslaved, they declared Cyrene free; and from that time forward it was a province of Rome. It was most likely for some share which Caius Marius had in robbing Egypt of this her most valuable province that he put the eagle and thunderbolt of the Ptolemies on one of his consular coins.

Goltzius,
de re Numm.

PTOLEMY SOTER II.

ON the flight of Alexander, the Alexandrians sent an embassy to Cyprus to bring back Soter II., or Lathyrus as he is called; and he entered Egypt without opposition. He had before reigned ten years with his mother, and then eighteen years by himself in Cyprus; and during those years of banishment had shown a wisdom and good behaviour which must have won the esteem of the Alexandrians when compared with his younger brother Alexander. He had held his ground against the fleets and armies of his mother, but either through weakness or good feeling had never invaded Egypt.

His reign is remarkable for the rebellion and ruin of the once powerful city of Thebes. It had long been falling in trade and in wealth, and had lost its superiority in arms; but its temples, like so many citadels, its obelisks, its colossal statues, and the tombs of its great kings, still remained, and with them the memory of its glory then gone by. The hieroglyphics on the walls still recounted, to its fallen priests and nobles, the provinces in Europe, Asia, and Africa which they once governed, and the weight of gold, silver, and corn which these provinces sent as a yearly tribute. The paintings and sculptures still showed the men of all nations and of all colours, from the Tartar of the north to the Negro of the south, who had graced the triumphs of their kings: and with these proud trophies before their eyes they had been bending under the yoke of Euergetes II. and Cleopatra Cocce for above fifty years.

Porphyrius, ap. Scalig. B.C. 87.

Tacitus, Annal. ii.

Rosellini.

Pausanias,
lib. i. 9.

We can therefore hardly wonder that, when Lathyrus landed in Egypt and tried to recall the troubled cities to quiet government and good order, Thebes should have refused to obey. For three years the brave Copts, intrenched within their temples, every one of which was a castle, withstood his armies; but the bows, the hatchets, and the chariots, could do little against Greek arms; while the overthrow of the massive temple walls, and the utter ruin of the city, prove how slowly they yielded to greater skill and numbers.

Perhaps the only time before when Thebes had been stormed after a long siege, was when it first fell under the Persians; and the ruin which marked the footsteps of Cambyses had never been wholly repaired. But the fierce and wanton cruelty of the foreigners did little mischief, when compared with the unpitying and

Denon.

unforgiving distrust of the native conquerors. The temples of Tentyra, Apollinopolis, Latopolis, and Philæ show that the massive Egyptian buildings can, when let alone, withstand the wear of time for thousands of years; but the harder hand of man works much faster, and the wide acres of Theban ruins prove alike the greatness of the city and the force with which it was overthrown: and this is the last time that Egyptian Thebes is met with in the pages of history.

The traveller now counts the Arab villages which stand within its bounds, and perhaps pitches his tent in the desert space in the middle of them. But the ruined temples still stand to call forth his wonder. They have seen the whole portion of time of which history keeps the reckoning roll before them: they have seeu kingdoms and nations rise and fall; the Babylonians, the Jews, the Persians, the Greeks, and the Romans. They have seen the childhood of all that we call ancient; and they still seem likely to stand, to tell their tale to those who will hereafter call us the ancients.

After this rebellion, Lathyrus reigned in quiet, and was even able to be of use to his Greek allies; and the Athenians, in gratitude, set up statues of bronze to him, and Berenice his daughter.

Pausanias, lib. i. 9.

During this reign, the Romans were carrying on a war with Mithridates, king of Pontus in Asia Minor, and they sent Lucullus as ambassador to Egypt to ask for help against their enemy. The whole Egyptian fleet moved out of harbour to meet him, a pomp which the kings of Egypt had before kept for themselves alone. Lathyrus received him on shore with the greatest respect, lodged him in the palace, and invited him to his own table, an honour which no foreigner had enjoyed since the kings of Egypt had thrown aside the plain manners of the first Ptolemies.

Plutarch. Lucullus.

Lucullus found time to enjoy the society of Dio, the academic philosopher, who was then teaching at Alexandria; and there he might have been seen with Antiochus of Athens, the pupil of Philo, and Heraclitus of Tyre, his fellow-pupil, talking together about the two newest works of Philo, which had just come to Alexandria. Antiochus could not read them without showing his anger : such opinions had never before been heard of in the Academy; but they knew the hand-writing of Philo, they were certainly his. Silius and Tetrilius, who were there, had heard him teach the same opinions at Rome, whither he had fled, and where he was then teaching Cicero. The next day, the matter was again talked over with Lucullus, Heraclitus, Aristus of Athens, Aristo of Cos, and Dio; and it ended in Antiochus writing a book, which he named Sosus, against those new opinions of his old master, against the new Academy, and in behalf of the old Academy.

Cicero, Acad. iv. 4.

Lathyrus was as much afraid of the enmity of Mithridates as of the Romans, and he wisely wished not to quarrel with either. He therefore at once made up his mind not to grant the fleet which

Plutarch. Lucullus.

Lucullus had been sent to ask for. It had been usual for the kings of Egypt to pay the expenses of the Roman ambassadors while living in Alexandria; and Lathyrus offered four times the usual allowance to Lucullus, beside eighty talents of silver. Lucullus, however, would take nothing beyond his expenses, and returned the gifts which were meant as a civil refusal of the fleet; and, having failed in his embassy, he sailed for Cyprus in a fleet of honour, carrying nothing with him but the king's portrait cut in an emerald.

Visconti,
Icon. Grec.

The coins of Lathyrus are not easily or certainly known from those of the other Ptolemies; but those of his second wife Selene bear her head on the one side, with the words ΒΑΣΙΛΙΣΣΗΣ ΣΕΛΗ-ΝΗΣ, '*of queen Selene*,' and on the other side the eagle, with the words ΒΑΣΙΛΕΩΣ ΠΤΟΛΕΜΑΙΟΥ, '*of king Ptolemy*.'

Porphyrius,
ap. Scalig.

He had before reigned ten years with his mother, and after his brother's death he reigned six years and a half more; but, as he counted the years that he had reigned in Cyprus, he died in the thirty-seventh year of his reign. He left a daughter named Berenice, and two natural sons, each named Ptolemy, one of whom reigned in Cyprus, and the other, nicknamed Auletes, *the piper*, afterwards gained the throne of Egypt.

CLEOPATRA BERENICE.

ON the death of Lathyrus, or Ptolemy Soter II., his daughter Cleopatra Berenice, the widow of Ptolemy Alexander, mounted the throne of Egypt; but it was also claimed by her step-son the young Alexander, who was then living in Rome.

Porphyrius, ap. Scalig. B.C. 80.

Alexander had been sent to the island of Cos, as a place of safety, when his grandmother Cleopatra Cocce followed her army into Cœlo-Syria. But, as the Egyptians had lost the command of the sea, the royal treasure in Cos was no longer out of danger, and the island was soon afterwards taken by Mithridates king of Pontus, who had conquered Asia Minor. Alexander fell into his hands; but he afterwards escaped, and reached the army of Sylla, under whose care he lived for some time in Rome. The Egyptian prince hoped to gain the throne of his father, by means of the friendship of one who could make and unmake kings at his pleasure; and Sylla might have thought that the wealth of Egypt would be at his command by means of his young friend. To these reasons Alexander added the bribe which was then becoming common with the princes who held their thrones by the help of Rome: he made a will, in which he named the Roman people as his heirs; and the senate then took care that the kingdom of Egypt should be a part of the wealth which was hereafter to be theirs by inheritance. After Berenice, his stepmother, had been queen about six months, they sent him to Alexandria, with orders that he should be received as king; and, to soften the harshness of this command, he was told to marry Berenice, and reign jointly with her.

Appianus, Bell.Civ.i.102.

Cicero, ii. contr. Rullum.

Porphyrius, ap. Scalig.

PTOLEMY ALEXANDER II.

B.C. 80. THE orders of Sylla, the Roman dictator, were of course obeyed, and the young Alexander landed at Alexandria, as king of Egypt,

Porphyrius, ap. Scalig. Cicero, frag. de rege Alex. Appian. Bell.Civ.i.102. and the friend of Rome. On the nineteenth day of his reign he married Berenice; and on the same day, with a cruelty unfortunately too common in this history, he put her to death. The marriage had been forced upon him by the Romans, who ordered all the political affairs of the kingdom; but, as they took no part in the civil or criminal affairs, he seems to have been at liberty to murder his wife. But Alexander was hated by the people as a king thrust upon them by foreign arms; and Berenice, whatever they might have before thought of her, was regretted as the queen of their choice. Hence his crime met with its just reward. His own guards immediately rose upon him: they dragged him from the palace to the gymnasium, and there put him to death.

Though the Romans had already seized the smaller kingdom of Cyrene, under the will of Ptolemy Apion, they could not agree among themselves upon the wholesale robbery of taking Egypt, Cicero, ii. contr. Rullum. under the will of Alexander. They seized, however, a paltry sum of money which he had left at Tyre as a place of safety; and it was a matter of debate for many years afterwards, in Rome, whether they should not claim the kingdom of Egypt. But the nobles of Rome, who sold their patronage to kings for sums equal to the revenues of provinces, would have lost much by handing the kingdom over to the senate. Hence the Egyptian monarchy was left standing for two reigns longer.

PTOLEMY NEUS DIONYSUS.

On the death of Ptolemy Alexander, the Alexandrians might easily have changed their weak and wicked rulers, and formed a government for themselves, if they had known how. But society is only held together by everybody believing that his neighbour will act fairly and justly, while more than usual self-denial, love of right, and trust in one another, are needed to form these bonds anew; and the whole of the scattered hints, which are all that is left to us of this history, show that those whose place in society had formed them to think and to be the leaders of their fellow citizens, wanted every virtue fitting for the task. B.C. 80.

As there was no other claimant, the crown fell to a natural son of Lathyrus. His claims had been wholly overlooked at the death of his father; for though by the Egyptian law every son was held to be equally legitimate, it was not so by the Macedonian law. He took the name of Neus Dionysus, or the young Osiris as we find it written in the hieroglyphics, though he is usually called Auletes, *the piper*; because he was more proud of his skill in playing on the flute than of his knowledge of the art of governing. Porphyrius, ap. Scalig. Egypt. Inscrip. plate 4.

From the first he gave himself up to his natural bent for pleasure and debauchery. At times when virtue is uncopied and unrewarded, it is usually praised and let alone; but in this reign sobriety was a crime in the eyes of the king, a quiet behaviour was thought a reproach against his irregularities. Demetrius the Platonic philosopher was in danger of being put to death because it Lucian. de Calumniâ.

was told to the king that he never drank wine, and had been seen at the feast of Bacchus in his usual dress, while every other man was in the dress of a woman. But the philosopher was allowed to disprove the charge of sobriety, or at least to make amends for his fault: on the king's sending for him the next day, he made himself drunk publicly in the sight of all the court, and danced with cymbals in a loose dress of Tarentine gauze.

Dion. Cass.
lib. xxxix.
As Auletes felt himself hardly safe upon the throne, his first wish was to get himself acknowledged as king by the Roman senate. For this end he sent to Rome a large sum of money to buy the votes of the senators. But though the Romans never tried to turn him out of his kingdom, it is uncertain how soon he got the wished-for decree, as we know nothing of the first twenty years of his reign.

Goltzius,
de re Numm.
B.C. 71.
On a coin of Lentulus Sura, who was consul in the tenth year of this reign, we find the Ptolemaic eagle and thunderbolt, as if he had been sent to Egypt by the senate to exercise some act of sovereignty; and on a coin of Licinius Crassus, who was consul the next year, we see a crocodile on one side and the prow of a ship on the other, which must be understood to mean that he had beaten the Egyptian fleet at the mouth of the Nile. Five years later we again meet with the eagle and thunderbolt on the consular coins of Aurelius Cotta, and we learn from Cicero that in that year it was found necessary to send a fleet to Alexandria to enforce the orders of the senate.

B. C. 65.

Cicero, ii.
contr. Rullum.

We next find the Roman senate debating whether they should not seize the kingdom as their inheritance under the will of Btolemy Alexander II., but, moved by the bribes of Auletes and perhaps by other reasons which we are not told, they seem to have acknowledged him as king.

But his brother Ptolemy who was reigning in Cyprus was not so well treated. They passed a law declaring that island a Roman province, no doubt upon the plea of the will of Ptolemy Alexander and the king's illegitimacy; and they sent Cato, rather against his wish, to turn him out of his kingdom. Ptolemy gave up the island without Cato being called upon to use force, and in return the Romans made him high-priest in the temple of the Paphian Venus; but he soon put himself to death by poison. Livy, Epit. civ.
B. C. 57.

Plutarch.
Cato.

Every thing, at least in this history, disproves the saying that the people are happy when their annals are short. There was more virtue and happiness, and perhaps even less bloodshed, with the stir of mind while Ptolemy Soter was at war with Antigonus, than during this dull unwarlike time. Auletes had been losing his friends and weakening his government, and at last, when he refused to quarrel with the senate about the island of Cyprus, the Egyptians rose against him in arms, and he was forced to fly from Alexandria. Dion. Cassius,
lib. xxxix.

He took ship for Rome, and in his way there he met Cato, who was at Rhodes on his voyage to Cyprus. He sent to Cato to let him know that he was in the city and that he wished to see him. But the Roman sent word back that he was unwell, and that if the king wanted to speak to him he must come himself. This was not a time for Auletes to quarrel with a senator, when he was on his way to Rome to beg for help against his subjects; so he was forced to go to the lodgings of Cato, who did not even rise from his seat when the king entered the room. But this treatment was not quite new to Auletes; in his flight from Alexandria in disguise and without a servant, he had known what it was to eat brown bread in the cottage of a peasant, and he now learned how much more irksome it was to wait upon the pleasure of a Roman senator. Plutarch.
Cato.

Cicero,
Tuscul. v. 34.

Plutarch.
Cato.

Cato gave him the best advice; that, instead of going to Rome, where he would find that all the wealth of Egypt would be thought a bribe too small for the greediness of the senators whose votes he wanted, he would do better to return to Alexandria and make peace with his rebellious subjects. Auletes however went on to Rome, and in the three years that he spent there in courting and bribing the senators, he learned the truth of Cato's advice.

Porphyrius,
ap. Scalig.

On the flight of their king, the Alexandrians set the two eldest of his daughters, Cleopatra Tryphæna and Berenice, on the throne, and sent an embassy, at the head of which was Dio the academic philosopher, to plead their cause at Rome against the king. But

Cicero, frag.
de rege Alex-
andrino.

the gold of Auletes had already gained the senate; and Cicero spoke, on his behalf, one of his great speeches, now unfortunately lost, in which he rebuts the charge that Auletes was at all to be blamed for the death of Alexander, whom he thought justly killed by his

Suetonius,
Cæsar, xi.
Plutarch.
Cæsar.

guards, for the murder of his queen and kinswoman. Cæsar, whose year of consulship was then drawing to an end, took his part warmly, and Auletes became in debt to him in the sum of seventeen million drachmæ, or about half a million sterling, either for money lent to bribe the senators, or for bonds then given to Cæsar instead of

Cicero,
pro Cœlio.

money. By these means, the door of the senate was shut against the Egyptian ambassadors, and Dio, the head of the embassy, was murdered in Rome. But nevertheless, Auletes was not able to get an army sent to help him against his daughters; nor was Cæsar able to get, for the employment of his proconsular year, the task of replacing Auletes on the throne.

Epist. ad Q.
Fratrem, ii. 2.

This high employment was then sought for by Lentulus and Pompey; and the senate at first leaned in favour of the former, who would perhaps have gained it, if the Roman creditors of Auletes, who were already trembling for their money, had not bribed openly in favour of Pompey, on whom the choice of the senate at last fell.

Pompey then took Auletes into his house, as his friend and guest, Dion. Cassius, lib. xxxix. and would perhaps have got orders to lead him back into his kingdom at the head of a Roman army, had not the tribunes of the people, fearing any addition to Pompey's great power, had recourse to their usual state-engine the Sibylline books; and the pontifex, at their bidding, publicly declared that it was written in those sacred pages that the king of Egypt should have the friendship of Rome, but should not be helped with an army.

But though Cæsar and Pompey were each strong enough to stop the other from having this high command, Auletes was not without hopes that some Roman general would be led, by the promise of money, and by the honour, to undertake his cause, though it would be against the laws of Rome to do so without orders from the senate. Cicero wrote to Lentulus, the proconsul of Cilicia, strongly urging Cicero, Epist. i. 7. him to snatch the glory of replacing Auletes on the throne, and of being the patron of the king of Egypt; but he seems not to have chosen to run the risk of so far breaking the laws of his country.

Auletes then went, with pressing letters from Pompey, to Gabinius, the proconsul of Syria, and offered him the large bribe of ten Dion Cass. lib. xxxix. Plutarch. Antony. thousand talents, or seventeen hundred thousand pounds, if he would lead the Roman army into Egypt, and replace him on the throne. Most of the officers were against this undertaking; but the letters of Pompey, the advice of Marc Antony the master of the horse, and perhaps the greatness of the bribe, outweighed those cautious opinions.

While Auletes had been thus pleading his cause at Rome and Porphyrius, ap. Scalig. with the army, Cleopatra Tryphæna, the elder of the two queens, had died; and, as no one of the other children of Auletes was old

Strabo,
lib. xvii.

enough to be joined with Berenice on the throne, the Alexandrians sent to Syria, to Seleúcus, the son of Antiochus Grypus and of Selene the sister of Lathyrus, to come to Egypt and marry Berenice.

He was low-minded in all his pleasures and tastes, and got the nickname of Cybiosactes, *the scullion.* He was even said to have stolen the golden sarcophagus in which the body of Alexander was buried; and was so much disliked by his young wife, that she had him strangled on the fifth day after their marriage.

Porphyrius,
ap. Scalig.

Berenice then married Archelaus, a son of Mithridates Eupator king of Pontus; and she had reigned one year with her sister, and two years with her husbands, when the Roman army brought back her father, Ptolemy Auletes, into Egypt.

Cicero,
pro Rabirio.

Plutarch.
Antony.

Gabinius, on marching, gave out as an excuse for quitting his province, that it was in self-defence; that Syria was in danger from the Egyptian fleet. Marc Antony was sent forward with the horse: he routed the Egyptian army near Pelusium, and then entered the city with Auletes. The king, in the cruelty of his revenge, wished to put the citizens to the sword, and was only stopt by Antony's forbidding it. On this first success, Gabinius followed with the body

Dion. Cass.
lib. xxxix.
Strabo, xvii..
B.C. 54.

of the army, and easily conquered the rest of the country, and then put to death Berenice and her husband Archelaus.

Cicero,
pro Rabirio.

Gabinius had refused to undertake this affair, which was the more dangerous because against the laws of Rome, unless the large bribe were first paid down in money. He would take no promises, and Auletes, who in his banishment had no money at his command, had to borrow it of some one who would listen to his large promises of after-payment. He found this person in Rabirius Posthumus, who had before lent him money, and who saw that it would be all lost unless Auletes regained the throne. Rabirius therefore lent him all he was worth, and borrowed the rest of his friends; and as soon as Auletes was on the throne, he went to Alexandria to claim his money and his reward. Auletes, who while he still stood in need of Roman help saw the advantage of keeping faith with his foreign creditors, at first gave Rabirius the office of royal *diœcetes*, or paymaster-general, which was one of great state and profit, and one by which he could in time have repaid himself his loan. But when the king felt safe upon his throne, he sent away his troublesome creditor, who returned to Rome with the loss of his money, to stand his trial for having lent it.

Rabirius had been for a time mortgagee in possession of the revenues of Egypt; and Auletes had felt more indebted for his crown to a Roman citizen than to the senate. But in the dealings of Rome with foreign kings, which were not unlike those of our East-India Company with the Indian nabobs, these evils had often before arisen and at last been made criminal; and while Gabinius was tried for treason, *de majestate*, for leading his army out of his province, Rabirius was tried, under the *Lex Julia de pecuniis repetundis*, for lending money and taking office under Auletes.

Cicero, ad Fratrem, iii. 1. pro Rabirio.

It was in this reign that the historian Diodorus Siculus travelled in Egypt, and wrote his account of the manners and religion of the people. What he tells us of the early Egyptian history is of little value, when compared with the histories of Manetho and of Eratosthenes, who were natives of the country and could read the hieroglyphical records, or even with that of Herodotus; but nevertheless he deserves great praise, and our warmest thanks, for being nearly the first Greek writer, when Egyptian learning could no longer be thought valuable; when the religion, though looked down upon, might at any rate be studied with ease,—for being nearly the first writer who thought the manners of this ancient people, after

Diod. Sic. lib. i. 83.

they had almost passed off the page of history, worth the notice of a philosopher.

Memphis was then a great city : in its crowded streets, its palaces and temples, it was second only to Alexandria. A little to the west stood the pyramids, which were thought one of the seven wonders of the world. Their broad bases, sloping sides, and solid masonry, had withstood the weather for ages ; and their huge unwieldy stones were a less easy quarry, for after builders, than the live rock when nearer to the river's side. The priests of Memphis knew the names of the kings who, one after the other, had built a new portico to their great temple of Pthah ; but as to the when, the why, or by whom the pyramids were built, they had as little to guide their guesses as we have.

The temple of Pthah, and every other building of Memphis, is now gone, and near the spot stands the great city of Caïro, whose mosques and minarets have been quarried out of its ruins. But the pyramids still stand unchanged, and almost unworn, and we still amuse ourselves with guessing by whom, and when, and why they were built.

One part of their task they have well fulfilled : they have outlived any portion of time that their builders could have dreamed of. But in another they seem to have failed : they have not yet unfolded to us their builders' names and history. The Thebans, more wisely, covered their buildings with writing ; but the unlettered people of the Delta, overlooking the reed which was growing in their marshes, the papyrus, to which the great minds of Greece afterwards trusted their undying names, have only taught us how much safer it would have been, in their wish to be thought of and talked of in after ages, to have leant upon the poet and historian.

The religion of the Copts was still flourishing. Though some of the temples of Lower Egypt had fallen into decay, and though the throne was then tottering to its fall, the priests in Upper Egypt were still building for immortality. The beautiful temples of Dendera and Esne, which were raised by the untiring industry of ages, and finished under the Roman emperors, were begun about this reign. A glance at that of Dendera, on which the earliest names are those of Cleopatra and her son Cæsarion, will show that time and the Greek government had made few changes in the form of an Egyptian temple.

The square low body of the temple is almost hid behind a portico, which is wider and loftier than the rest, and is itself nearly one half of the building, and which shows a front of six thick columns, each having the head of a woman for its capital. All the massive walls slope a little inwards, which adds both to the strength and to the appearance of it. They are covered with hieroglyphics, but are otherwise plain, without window, niche, or any ornament but the deep overshadowing eaves of the roof. On entering the portico, you see that its ceiling is upheld by twenty-four columns, in four rows of six each; you thence enter the body of the temple, through a doorway, into the chief room, where there are six more columns, and, passing straight forward through two other rooms, you reach the fourth and last, leaving several smaller rooms on each side. The larger temples of Thebes were in most part open to the sky; but this seems to have been wholly roofed, except the middle of the chief room. Every part is small after the spacious portico; and the whole seems planned as much for strength as for beauty, as much for a castle as for a temple. In front of the portico there may have been once a walled court-yard; but its massive doorway is the only part which is now standing.

Denon,
pl. 38, 39, 40.

Diod. Sic.
lib. i. 84.

The sacred animals were still kept by the several cities, and their funerals were celebrated with great pomp, particularly that of the bull Apis; and at a cost, in one case, of one hundred talents, or seventeen thousand pounds; which was double what Ptolemy Soter, in his wish to please his new subjects, spent upon the Apis of his day. After the funeral the priests looked for a calf with the right spots, a custom which must have been older than the time of Moses, as the Jews were by him ordered to choose a red heifer without a spot. When they had chosen the calf they fattened it for forty days, and brought it to Memphis in a boat under a golden awning, and lodged it safely in the temple.

Numbers,
xix. 2.

The cat also was at all times one of the animals held most sacred by the Egyptians. In the earliest and latest times we find the statues of their goddesses with cats' heads; and when the cats of Alexandria were looked upon as so many images of Neith or the Minerva of Sais, a goddess worshipped both by Greeks and Egyptians, it passed into a proverb with the Greeks, when they spoke of any two things being unlike, to say that they were as much like one another as a cat was to Minerva.

British
Museum.

Plutarch.
Proverbia
Alexandrina.

It is to Alexandria also that we trace the story of a cat turned into a lady to please a prince who had fallen in love with it. The lady, however, when dressed in her bridal robes, could not help scampering round the room after a mouse seen upon the floor; and when Plutarch was in Egypt it had already become a proverb, that any one in too much finery was as awkward as a cat in a crocus-coloured robe.

Diod. Sic.
lib. i. 83.

So deeply rooted in the minds of the Egyptians was the worship of these animals, that when a Roman soldier had killed a cat unawares, though the Romans were masters of the country, the whole of the people rose against him in a fury. In vain the king sent a message to quiet the mob, to let them know that the cat was killed by accident; and though the fear of Rome would most likely have saved a Roman soldier unharmed, whatever other crime he might have been guilty of, in this case nothing would quiet the people but his death, and he was killed before the eyes of Diodorus the historian.

One nation rises above another not so much from its greater strength or skill in arms as from its higher aim and stronger wish for power. The Egyptians, we see, had not lost their courage, and when the occasion called them out they showed a fearlessness not unworthy of their Theban forefathers; on seeing a dead cat in the streets they rose against the king's orders and the power of Rome; had they thought their own freedom or their country's greatness as much worth fighting for, they could with ease have gained them.

But the Egyptians had no civil laws or rights that they cared about, they had nothing left that they valued but their religion, and this the Romans took good care not to meddle with. Had the Romans made war upon the priests and temples as the Persians had done, they would perhaps in the same way have been driven out of Egypt; but they never shocked the religious feelings of the people, and even after Egypt had become a Roman province, when the beautiful temples of Esne, Dendera, and other cities, were dedicated in the names of the Roman emperors, they never once copied the example of Philometor, and put Greek, much less Roman writing on the portico, but continued to let the walls be covered with hieroglyphical inscriptions.

Every Egyptian, who was rich enough to pay for it, still had the bodies of his friends embalmed at their death, and made into mummies; though the priests, to save part of the cost, often put the mummy of a man just dead into a mummy-case which had been

Diod. Sic. lib. i. 92.

Archæologia, xxvii. 262.

made and used in the reign of a Thothmothis or an Amunothph.
When the mummy was finished, it was part of the funeral to ferry
it across a lake, and there before a judge, and a jury of forty-two,
to try the dead man for what he had done when living.

But human nature is the same in all ages and in all countries,
and, whatever might have been the past life of the dead, the judge,
not to hurt the feelings of the friends, always declared that he was
Plutarch.
Prov. Alex. ' a righteous good man :' and, notwithstanding this show of truth,
it passed into a proverb to say of a wicked man, that he was too
bad to be praised even at his funeral.

Though the old laws of Egypt must very much have fallen into
disuse during the reigns of the latter Ptolemies, they had at least
been left unchanged ; and they teach us that the shadow of freedom may be seen, as in Rome under the Cæsars, and in Florence
Diod. Sic.
lib. i. 73, 75. under the Medici, long after the substance has been lost. In quarrels between man and man, the thirty judges, from the cities of
Thebes, Memphis, and Heliopolis, were still guided by the eight
books of the law. The king, the priests, and the soldiers were the
only landholders in the country, while the herdsmen, husbandmen,
and handicraftsmen were thought of lower caste. Though the armies of Egypt were for the most part filled with Greek mercenaries,
and the landholders of the order of soldiers could then have had
as little to do with arms as knights and esquires have in our days,
yet they still boasted of the wisdom of their laws, by which arms
were only to be trusted to men who had a stake in the country
worth fighting for.

We may form some opinion of the wealth of Egypt in its more
Strabo, xvii. prosperous times, when we learn from Cicero that in this reign,
when the Romans had good means of knowing, the revenues of
the country amounted to twelve thousand five hundred talents, or

two millions sterling; just one half of which was paid by the port Diod. Sic. lib. xvii. 52. of Alexandria. This was at a time when the foreign trade had, through the faults of the government, sunk down to its lowest ebb, when not more than twenty ships sailed each year from the Red Sea to India; when the population of the kingdom had so far fallen off that it was not more than three millions, which was only lib. i. 31. half of what it had been in the reign of Ptolemy Soter, though lib. xvii. 52. Alexandria alone still held three hundred thousand persons.

But though much of the trade of the country was lost, though lib. iii. 12. many of the royal works had ceased, though the manufacture of the finer linen had left the country, the digging in the gold mines, the only source of wealth to a despot, never ceased. Night and day in the mines near Berenice did slaves, criminals, and prisoners of war work without pause, chained together in gangs, and guarded by soldiers, who were carefully chosen for their not being able to speak the language of these unhappy workmen.

The rock which held the gold was broken up into small pieces; when hard, it was first made brittle in the fire; the broken stone was then washed to separate the waste from the heavier grains which held the gold; and, lastly, the valuable parts when separated were kept heated in a furnace for five days, at the end of which time the pure gold was found melted into a button at the bottom. We are not told the value of the gold, but it must have been a very small part of the seven millions sterling which the mines are said to have yielded every year in the reign of Rameses II.

As the country fell off in wealth, power, and population, the schools of Alexandria fell off in learning, and we meet with few authors whose names can brighten the pages of this reign. Apol- Ant. Cocchius, Chirurg. Græc. lonius of Cittium, indeed, who had studied surgery and anatomy at Alexandria under Zopyrus, when he returned to Cyprus, wrote a treatise on the joints of the body, and dedicated his work to Ptolemy king of that island. The work is still remaining in manuscript, though unpublished. But so few are the deeds worth mentioning in the falling state, that we are pleased even to be told that,

Pausanias, lib. v. 21. in the one hundred and seventy-eighth Olympiad, Straton of Alexandria conquered in the Olympic games, and was crowned in the same day for wrestling, and for *pancratium*, or wrestling and boxing joined.

Hieroglyphics, plate 65. Beside his name of Neus Dionysus, the king is in the hieroglyphics sometimes called Philopator and Philadelphus; and in a

Inscript. Letronne, Recherch. 134. Greek inscription on a statue at Philæ he is called by the three names, Neus Dionysus, Philopator, Philadelphus.

Visconti, Icon. Grec. The coins which are usually thought to be his are in a worse style of art than those of the kings before him.

Porphyrius, ap. Scalig. He died in the twenty-ninth year of his reign, leaving four children; namely, Cleopatra, Arsinoë, and two Ptolemies.

CLEOPATRA.

PTOLEMY AULETES had by his will left his kingdom to Cleopatra and Ptolemy, his elder daughter and elder son, who, agreeably to the custom of the country, were to marry one another and reign with equal power. He had sent one copy of his will to Rome, to be lodged in the public treasury, and in it he called upon the Roman people, by all the gods and by the treaties by which they were bound, to see that his will was obeyed.

J. Cæsar,
Bell. Civ. iii.
B.C. 51.

He had also begged them to undertake the guardianship of his son, and the senate voted Pompey tutor to the young king, or governor of Egypt. But the power of Pompey was by that time at an end, and the votes of the senate could give no power to the weak; hence the eunuch Photinus, who had the care of the elder Ptolemy, was governor of Egypt, and his first act was to declare his young pupil king, and to set at nought the will of Auletes, by which Cleopatra was joined with him on the throne.

Eutropius,
lib. vi. 21.

J. Cæsar,
Bell. Civ. iii.

Cleopatra fled into Syria, and, with a manly spirit which showed what she was afterwards to be, raised an army and marched back to the borders of Egypt, to claim her rights by force of arms. It was in the second year of her reign, when the Egyptian forces were moved to Pelusium to meet her, and the two armies were within a few leagues of one another, that Pompey, who had been the friend of Auletes when the king wanted a friend, landed on the shores of Egypt in distress, and almost alone. His army had just been beaten at Pharsalia, and he was flying from Cæsar, and he

B.C. 49.

J. Cæsar,
Bell. Civ. iii.
hoped to receive from the son the kindness which he had shown to the father.

But gratitude is a virtue little known to princes, and Pompey's heart misgave him as he stept into the Egyptian vessel which was sent out to receive him with promises of safety and kind treatment. In this civil war between Pompey and Cæsar, the Egyptians would have been glad to be the friends of both, but that was now out of the question; Pompey's coming made it necessary for them to choose which they should join, and the council of Ptolemy chose to side with the strong, and though they had just given to Pompey a promise of safety they put him to death on his landing.

Shortly after this, Cæsar landed at Alexandria, and brought with him only the small force of three thousand two hundred foot and eight hundred horse, that he might be the less hindered in his pursuit of Pompey, trusting that the news of his victory at Pharsalia would make a larger force unnecessary. He found the citizens in a state of disorder, which was not a little increased by his entering the city as a master, with the lictors marching before him, carrying the fasces as the mark of his rank. It was not till after some days that the city was quieted, and he would even have withdrawn for safety if the winds had not made it difficult to quit the harbour. He sent, however, a message for the legions which he had left in Asia, to come to him as soon as they could.

In the mean while he claimed the right, as Roman consul, of settling the dispute between Cleopatra and her brother, and though he had only four thousand men himself, he ordered them both to disband their armies. Ptolemy, who was at Alexandria, seemed willing to obey, but Photinus his guardian would not agree to it, and secretly sent orders to Achillas, the general at Pelusium, to bring the army to Alexandria, that they might be able to give orders rather than to receive them from Cæsar and his four thousand men. On the other hand Ptolemy, at the command of Cæsar, sent Dioscorides and Serapion to order Achillas to remain at Pelusium ; but these messengers were not even allowed to return, one was killed and the other badly wounded, and Achillas entered Alexandria at the head of twenty thousand foot and two thousand horse.

Cæsar, during the few days that he had been in Alexandria, had made many enemies by claiming the large debt which was due to him from Auletes the late king. Photinus, who as treasurer collected the tribute and paid it to him, carefully made the demands appear as harrassing as he could ; hence, when Achillas entered Alexandria at the head of his large army, Cæsar had no party in the city, and had only his own little body of troops to trust to.

Plutarch.
Cæsar.

He took with him the two young Ptolemies, their sister Arsinoë, and the minister Photinus, as hostages for his own safety, and shut himself up in one quarter of the city with the harbour on one side and the palace as a chief fortress. The strong walls of the palace easily withstood the attacks of Achillas, and Cæsar's brave and well-trained little band drove back the larger forces which crowded one another in the narrow streets. The greatest struggle was near the harbour, and if Cæsar had lost his gallies he would have been beaten. But the Romans fought in despair, and he was able to burn all the gallies which he could not guard, as well as those in the docks ; and by these means he kept the harbour and the island of Pharos, which commands the mouth.

J. Cæsar,
Bell. Civ. iii.

But unfortunately the fire did not stop at the gallies ; from the docks it caught the neighbouring buildings, and the Museum which was close upon the harbour was soon wrapt in flames. It was to the Museum with its seven hundred thousand volumes, that Alexandria owed much of its renown, and it is for the men of letters

Amm. Marcel.
lib. xxii. 16.

who had studied there that the history of the Ptolemies is chiefly valuable. It had been begun by the first of the Lagidæ, and had grown not only with his son and grandson, but, when the love of learning and of virtue had left the latter princes of the family, they still added to the library, and Alexandria was still the first school of science, and, next to Athens, the point to which all men of learning looked.

Cæsar, the historian of his own great deeds, could have told us of the pain with which he saw the flames rise from the rolls of dry papyrus, and of the trouble which he took to quench the fire; but his guilty silence leads us to believe that he found the burning pile a useful flank to the line of walls that his little body of troops had to guard, and we must fear that the feelings of the scholar were for the time lost in those of the soldier.

J. Cæsar,
Bell. Civ. iii.

He must have known that, in keeping the young princes and their guardian, he was keeping traitors in his camp. This was first shown by Arsinoë making her escape from the palace, and reaching the quarters of Achillas in safety; and then by Photinus being found out in sending word to Achillas of Cæsar's want of stores, and in urging him not to give over his attacks upon the palace.

A. Hirtius,
Bell. Alex.

Upon this Cæsar put Photinus to death, and the escape of Arsinoë soon turned out a gain, as she quarrelled with Achillas the general, and had him murdered by her eunuch Ganimedes.

Plutarch.
Cæsar.

Cleopatra was all this time with her army near Pelusium, but believing that her charms would have more weight with Cæsar, in his judging between herself and her brother, than any thing that she could say by letter, she came in disguise with one friend to Alexandria, and reached the palace in safety. She at once threw herself upon Cæsar, and was not mistaken in the strength that her cause would gain from her youth and beauty; and though he had before ordered that she should obey her father's will, and reign jointly with her brother, she found herself mistress of his heart, and through him of the kingdom of Egypt.

On this, Ptolemy joined the army against Cæsar, and after a year and a half's fighting, during which time Cæsar had been strengthened by the arrival of an army under Mithridates of Pergamus, Ptolemy was wholly beaten, and at last drowned by the sinking of his vessel in the harbour of Alexandria, in the fourth year after the death of Auletes. Arsinoë was then declared queen by the Egyptian army, but she was taken prisoner by Cæsar with her eunuch Ganimedes; and Cæsar, still following the will of Auletes, declared the younger Ptolemy, a boy of eleven years of age, joint sovereign with Cleopatra, and, after having been two years in Alexandria, he quitted Egypt with his prisoner Arsinoë, leaving Cleopatra, who had just borne him a son named Cæsarion, quietly seated on the throne.

On reaching Rome he struck a coin with a crocodile on it, and the words ÆGYPTO CAPTA, in boast of his victory; and he amused the people and himself with a grand triumphal show, in which, among the other prisoners of war, the princess Arsinoë followed his car in chains; and, among the works of art and nature which were got together to prove to the gazing crowd the greatness of his conquests, was that remarkable African animal the camelopard, then for the first time seen in Rome. Nor was this the last of Cæsar's triumphs, for soon afterwards Cleopatra and her brother Ptolemy, then twelve years old, who was called her husband, came to Rome as his guests, and dwelt for some time with him in his house.

While Ptolemy her second husband was a boy, and could claim no share of the government, he was allowed to live with all the

Margin notes:
A. Hirtius, Bell. Alex.

B.C. 47.

Goltzius, de re Numm. Dion. Cassius. lib. xliii.

Porphyrius, ap. Scalig.

outward show of royalty, but as soon as he reached the age of fifteen, at which he might call himself the equal and would soon be the master of Cleopatra, she had him put to death. She had then reigned four years with her elder brother, and four years with her younger brother, and from that time forward she reigned alone.

B.C. 43.

At a time when vice and luxury claimed the thoughts of all who were not busy in the civil wars, we cannot hope to find the fruits of genius in Alexandria; but the mathematics are plants of a hardy growth, and are not choked so easily as poetry and history. Sosigenes was then the first astronomer in Egypt, and Julius Cæsar was guided by his advice in setting right the Roman Calendar. He was a careful and painstaking mathematician, and, after fixing the length of the year at three hundred and sixty-five days and a quarter, he three times changed the beginning of the year, in his doubts as to the day on which the equinox fell; for the astronomer could then only make two observations in a year with a view to learn the time of the equinox, by seeing when the sun shone in the plane of the equator.

Pliny, lib. xviii. 57.

Suidas.

Didymus was another of the writers that we hear of at that time. He was a man of great industry, both in reading and writing; but when we are told that he wrote three thousand five hundred volumes, or rolls, it rather teaches us that a great many rolls of papyrus would be wanted to make a modern book, than what number of books he wrote.

Dioscorides, the physician of Cleopatra, has left a work on herbs and minerals, and on their uses in medicine; also on poisons and poisonous bites. To these he has added a list of prescriptions. His works have been much read in all ages, and have only been set aside by the discoveries of the last few centuries.

Serapion was another physician of this reign. He followed me- Celsus, lib. i.
dicine rather than surgery; and, while trusting chiefly to his experience gained in clinical or bed-side practice, was laughed at by the
surgeons as an empiric.

The small temple at Hermonthis, near Thebes, seems to have Wilkinson's
Thebes.
been built in this reign, and it is dedicated to Mandoo, or the sun,
by Cleopatra and Cæsarion. It is unlike the older Egyptian temples Denon, pl. 51.
in being much less of a fortress; for what in them is a strongly-
walled court-yard, with towers to guard the narrow doorway, is here
a small space between two double rows of columns, wholly open,
without walls, while the roofed building is the same as in the older
temples. Near it is a small pool, seventy feet square, with stone
sides, which was most likely used in the funerals and other religious
rites.

Although the history of Egypt, at this time, is almost lost in that
of Rome, we must not be led too far out of our path. It is enough
to say that within five years of Cæsar's landing in Alexandria, and
finding that, by the death of Pompey, he was master of the world,
he paid his own life as the forfeit for making himself the autocrat
of Rome. But the murder of Cæsar did not raise the character of
the Romans, or make them more fit for self-government; and
when, by the battle of Philippi and the death of Brutus and Cassius,
his party was again uppermost, the Romans willingly bowed their
necks to his adopted son Octavianus, and his friend Marc Antony.

As Antony was passing through Cilicia with his army, he sent Plutarch.
Antony.
B.C. 42.
orders to Cleopatra to come from Egypt and meet him at Tarsus,
to answer the charge of having helped Brutus and Cassius in the
late war. Dellius, the bearer of the message, soon showed that he
understood the meaning of it, by beginning himself to pay court to
her as his queen. He advised her to go, like Juno, 'tricked in her

best attire,' and told her that she had nothing to fear from the kind and gallant Antony. On this, she sailed for Cilicia in the full trust in her beauty and power of pleasing. She had won the heart of Cæsar when, though younger, she was less skilled in the arts of love; and she was still only twenty-five years old, and carrying with her such gifts and treasures as became her rank, she entered the river Cydnus in the Egyptian fleet:

Shakspeare,
from Plutarch.

> The barge she sat in, like a burnish'd throne,
> Burn'd on the water: the poop was beaten gold,
> Purple the sails, and so perfumed, that
> The winds were love-sick with them; the oars were silver,
> Which to the tune of flutes kept stroke, and made
> The water which they beat to follow faster,
> As amorous of their strokes. For her own person,
> It beggar'd all description. She did lie
> In her pavilion, cloth of gold, of tissue,
> O'er-picturing that Venus, where we see
> The fancy outwork nature; on each side her
> Stood pretty dimpled boys, like smiling Cupids,
> With divers-coloured fans.—
>   Her gentlewomen, like the Nereids,
> So many mermaids, tended her i' the eyes
> And made their bends adornings; at the helm
> A seeming mermaid steers; the silken tackle
> Swell with the touches of those flower-soft hands,
> That yarely frame the office. From the barge,
> A strange invisible perfume hits the sense
> Of the adjacent wharfs. The city cast
> Her people out upon her; and Antony,
> Enthroned in the market-place, did sit alone.

On her landing, she invited him and his generals to a dinner, at Athenæus, lib. iv. 11. which the whole of the dishes placed before him were of gold, set with precious stones, and the room and the twelve couches were ornamented with purple and gold. On Antony's praising the splendour of the sight, as passing any thing he had before seen, she said it was a trifle, and begged that he would take the whole of it as a gift from her.

The next day he again dined with her, and brought a larger number of his friends and generals, and was of course startled to see a costliness which made that of the day before seem nothing; and she again gave him the whole of the gold upon the table, and gave to each of his friends the couch upon which he sat.

These costly and delicate dinners were continued every day; and Pliny, lib. ix. 58. one evening, when Antony playfully blamed her wastefulness, and said that it was not possible to fare in a more costly manner, she told him that the dinner of the next day should cost ten thousand sestertia, or sixty thousand pounds sterling. This he would not believe, and laid her a wager that she would fail in her promise.

Next day the dinner was as grand and dainty as those of the former days; but when Antony called upon her to count up the cost of the meats and wines, she said that she did not reckon them, but that she should herself soon eat and drink the ten thousand sestertia.

She wore in her ears two pearls, the largest known in the world, which, like the diamonds of European kings, had come to her with her crown and kingdom, and were together valued at that large sum. On the servants removing the meats, they set before her a glass of vinegar, and she took one of these ear-rings from her ear and dropt it into the glass, and when dissolved drank it off. Plancus, one of the guests, who had been made judge of the wager.

snatched the other from the queen's ear, and saved it from being drunk up like the first, and then declared that Antony had lost his bet. The pearl which was saved was afterwards cut in two, and made into a pair of ear-rings for the statue of Venus in the Pantheon at Rome; and the fame of the wager may be said to have made the two half pearls at least as valuable as the two whole ones.

Plutarch.
Antony. The beauty, sweetness, and gaiety of this young queen, joined to her great powers of mind, which were all turned to the art of pleasing, had quite overcome Antony: he had sent for her as her master, but he was now her slave. She sang beautifully; she spoke readily to every ambassador in his own language; and was said to be the only sovereign of Egypt who could understand the languages of all her subjects: Greek, Egyptian, Ethiopic, Troglodytic, Hebrew, Arabic, and Syriac. With these charms, at the age of five-and-twenty, the luxurious Antony could deny her nothing.

Josephus,
Antiq. xv. 4. The first favour which she asked of her lover equals any cruelty that we have met with in this history: it was, that he would have her sister Arsinoë put to death. Cæsar had spared her life, after his triumph, through love of Cleopatra; but he was mistaken in the heart of his mistress, she would have been then better pleased at Arsinoë's death; and Antony, at her bidding, had her murdered in the temple of Diana at Ephesus.

Plutarch.
Antony. Though Fulvia, the faithful wife of Antony, could scarcely keep together his party at Rome, against the power of Octavianus his colleague in the triumvirate, and though Labienus, with the Parthian legions, was ready to march into Syria against him, yet he was so entangled in the artful nets of Cleopatra, that she led him captive to Alexandria, where the old warrior fell into every idle amusement, and offered up, at the shrine of pleasure, one of the greatest of sacrifices, the sacrifice of his time.

The lovers visited each other every day, and the waste of their entertainments passed belief. Philotas, a physician who was then following his studies at Alexandria, told Plutarch's grandfather that he once saw Antony's dinner cooked, and, among other meats, were eight wild boars roasting whole; and the cook explained to him that, though there were only twelve guests, yet as each dish had to be roasted to a single turn of the spit, and Antony did not know at what hour he should dine, it was necessary to cook at least eight dinners.

But the most costly of the luxuries then used in Egypt were the scents and the ointments. Gold, silver, and jewels, as Pliny remarks, will pass to a man's heirs, even clothes will last a few months or weeks, but scents fly off and are lost at the first moment that they are admired; and yet ointments, like the attar of roses, which melted and gave out their scent, and passed into air when placed upon the back of the hand, as the coolest part of the body, were sold for four hundred denarii the pound.

Pliny, lib. xiii. 3, 4.

Cleopatra, who held her power at the pleasure of the Roman legions, spared no pains to please Antony. She had borne him first a son, and then a son and a daughter, twins. She gamed, she drank, she hunted, she reviewed the troops with him, and she followed him in his midnight rambles through the city; and nothing that youth, beauty, wealth, and elegance could do to throw a cloak over the grossness of vice and crime, was forgotten by her. But in the middle of this gaiety and feasting, he was recalled to Europe, by letters which told him that his wife and brother had been driven out of Rome by Octavianus.

Plutarch. Antony.

In the next year, however, he was again in Syria, and he sent to Alexandria to beg Cleopatra to join him there. On her coming, he made her perhaps the largest gift which lover ever gave to his mistress: he gave her the wide provinces of Phenicia, Cœlo-Syria, Cyprus, part of Cilicia, part of Judæa, and part of Arabia Nabatæa.

Josephus, Bell. Jud. lib. i. 13, 15.
These large gifts only made her ask for more, and she begged him to put to death Herod king of Judæa, and Malichus king of Arabia Nabatæa, the former of whom had advised Antony to break through the disgraceful ties which bound him to Cleopatra, as the only means of saving himself from being crushed by the rising power of Octavianus. But Antony had not so far forgotten himself as to yield to these commands; and he only gave her the balsam country round Jericho, and a rent-charge of two hundred talents, or three thousand five hundred pounds, a year, on the revenues of Judæa.

Porphyrius, ap. Scalig.
On receiving this large addition to her kingdom, and perhaps in honour of Antony, who had then lost all power in Italy but was the real king of Egypt and its Greek provinces, Cleopatra began to count the years of her reign afresh: what was really the sixteenth of her reign she called the first, and reckoned them in the same way till her death.

Vaillant, Hist. Ptolem.
On the early coins of Cleopatra we see her head on the one side and the eagle or the cornucopia on the other side, with the words ΒΑΣΙΛΙΣΣΗΣ ΚΛΕΟΠΑΤΡΑΣ, '*of queen Cleopatra.*' On the later coins we find the head of Antony joined with hers, as king and queen, with the words, ΑΥΤΟΚΡΑΤѠΡ, '*emperor,*' and ΘΕΑ ΝΕѠΤΕΡΑ, '*the young goddess.*' After she had borne him children, we find the words round their heads, ANTONI ARMENIA DEVICTA, '*of Antony, on the conquest of Armenia*; CLEOPATRÆ REGINÆ REGVM FILIORVM REGVM, '*of Cleopatra the queen, and of the kings the children of kings.*'

Plutarch. Antony.
But after wondering at the wasteful feasts and gifts, in which pearls and provinces were alike trifled with, we are reminded that even Cleopatra was of the family of the Lagidæ, and that she was

well aware how much the library of the Museum had added to the glory of Alexandria. It had been burnt by the Roman troops under Cæsar, and, to make amends for this, Antony gave her the large library of the city of Pergamus, by which Eumenes and Attalus had hoped to raise a school that should equal the Museum of Alexandria. Cleopatra placed these two hundred thousand volumes in the temple of Serapis, and Alexandria again held the largest library in the world.

By the help of this new library, the city still kept its high rank as a school of letters; and when the once proud kingdom of Egypt was a province of Rome, and when almost every trace of the monarchy was lost, and centuries after Philo the Jewish philosopher of Alexandria had asked, 'Where are now the Ptolemies?' the historian could have found an answer by pointing to the mathematical schools and the library of the Serapeum. Philo de Jos.

With whom the blame should rest for the loss of these valuable books we do not well know. Many seem to have been destroyed when the temple of Serapis was attacked by the Christians in the fourth century, and Orosius tells us that he then saw the empty shelves. All that escaped these quarrels, or were afterwards added, were burnt when the city was taken by the Arabs in the seventh century. Orosius, lib. iv. 15.

The Arabic historian tells us that, when Alexandria opened its gates to the army of Amru Ben al Aas, he set his seal upon all the public property in the city. But John, a learned grammarian, who though he had lost his rank in the church because he would not receive the trinitarian faith has gained the thanks of every friend to knowledge, begged that the books might be left in the public library, as they would be of no use to the conquerors. Amru, a man of kind feelings and good sense, would have granted this Abul-Pharagius, Dyn. ix.

favour if he had not thought it necessary to ask leave of the Calif.
He therefore wrote to Omar for orders, who answered him, that if
the books were the same as the Coran they were useless, but if
not the same, they were worse than useless; and that in either
Abdollatif,
cap. iv. case they were to be burnt. Amru obeyed this order, and sent the
books, most of which were of papyrus, to the public baths of Alexandria, which were heated with them for the space of six months.

In weighing the loss that befel the world in the burning of
these great libraries, that of the Museum and that of the Serapeum,
or as they should perhaps be called that of Alexandria and that of
Pergamus, we must remember that by no care could the manuscripts have escaped the wear and tear of time, and lived till printing
came into use. We have very few manuscripts on vellum more
than a thousand years old, and most of those volumes were written
on papyrus, a much less lasting substance. Hence we must think
only of what the men of learning then lost, and of the copies that
might have been made from them.

When Egypt was conquered by the Arabs in the seventh century, and the schools of Alexandria were overthrown, and the books
fell into the hands of men with so little knowledge that they could
burn them, we see at once that we should have gained little by
their being left unhurt, but at the same time unread and uncopied.
And though it was otherwise when the library of the Museum was
burnt by Julius Cæsar, when the schools, crowded with foreign
students, were at once robbed of their books, and the writers, who
were there earning their livelihood by copying, were at once stopped
in their work, yet the loss was more easily repaired from the other
copies in the hands of the learned. Upon the whole it may perhaps be shown that the loss to the world of the numerous valuable
Greek works is more owing to the cloud of darkness which over-

spread Europe in the middle ages, than to any such accidents; yet when we read of the beauties of the poets and orators now lost, and of the historians who could have filled up for us the great gaps which disfigure history, the student cannot help setting down much of his loss to the burning of these great libraries in Alexandria.

But to return to our history. When Antony left Cleopatra, he marched against the Parthians, and on his return he again entered Alexandria in triumph, and soon afterwards made known his plans for the government of Egypt and the provinces. *Plutarch. Antony.*

He called together the Alexandrians, and seating himself and Cleopatra on two golden thrones, he declared her son Cæsarion her colleague, and that they should hold Egypt, Cyprus, Africa, and Cœlo-Syria. To each of her sons by himself he gave the title of king; and to Alexander, the elder, though still a child, he gave Armenia and Media, with Parthia when it should be conquered; and to the younger he gave Phenicia, Syria, and Cilicia; and to Cleopatra he also gave the whole of his Parthian booty, and his prisoner Tigranes, the son of the Parthian king. *Josephus, Bell. Jud. lib. i. 13.*

The death of Julius Cæsar and afterwards of Brutus and Cassius had left Antony with the chief sway in the Roman world; but his life of pleasure in Egypt had done much to forfeit it, and Octavianus, afterwards called Augustus, had been for some time rising in power against him. His party however was still strong enough in Rome to choose for consul his friend Sosius, who put the head of Antony on one side of his coins, and the Egyptian eagle and thunderbolt on the other. Soon afterwards Antony was himself chosen as consul elect for the coming year, and he then struck the last coins of which Egypt can boast. One in silver has round his head the words *Plutarch. Antony.* *Goltzius, de re Numm.*

IMP. ANTON. AVG. IMP. IIII. COS. DES. III. III. VIR. II. R. P. C.

'*The Imperator Antony, Augur, Imperator a fourth time, Consul elect a third time, Triumvir a second time*; *on the concord of the republic*;' and on the other side is a palm tree with the words

British
Museum.

ALEXANDR. AEGYPT; while the rude copper coins have on one side the words BACIΛ. ΘEA. NE. '*The queen, the young goddess*'; and on the other side ANTω. ΥΠΑ. Γ. '*Antony consul a third time.*' But he never was consul for the third time; before the day of entering on the office war was declared against him by Octavianus.

Plutarch.
Antony.

At the beginning of the year which was to end with the battle of Actium, Octavianus held Italy, Gaul, Spain, and Carthage, with an army of eighty thousand foot, twelve thousand horse, and a fleet of two hundred and fifty ships: Antony held Egypt and Cyrene, with one hundred thousand foot, twelve thousand horse, and five hundred ships; he was followed by the kings of Africa, Cilicia, Cappadocia, Paphlagonia, and Thrace, and he received help from the kings of Pontus, Arabia, Judæa, Lycaonia, and Galatia. Thus Octavianus held Rome, with its western provinces, and hardy legions, while Antony held the Greek kingdom of Ptolemy Philadelphus. But the mind of Antony was weakened by his life of pleasure. He even carried with him into battle his beloved Cleopatra, 'the

Lucanus,
lib. x. 59.

republic's firebrand, Egypt's foul disgrace,' and was beaten at sea by Octavianus, on the coast of Epirus, near Actium. This battle, which sealed the fate of Antony, of Egypt, and of Rome, would never have been spoken of in history if he had then had the courage to join his land forces; but he sailed away in a fright to Alexandria, with Cleopatra, leaving an army larger than that of Octavianus, which would not believe that he was gone.

Plutarch.
Antony.

In Alexandria, Antony and Cleopatra only so far regained their courage as to forget their losses, and to plunge into the same round of costly feasts and shows that they had amused themselves with before their fall: but while they were wasting these few weeks in pleasure, Octavianus was moving his fleet and army upon Egypt.

When he landed on the coast, Egypt held three millions of people; he might have been met by three hundred thousand men able to bear arms. As for money, which has sometimes been called the sinews of war, though there might have been none in the treasury, yet it could not have been wanting in Alexandria. But the Egyptians, like the ass in the fable, had nothing to fear from a change of masters; they could hardly be kicked and cuffed worse than they had been; and, though they themselves were the prize struggled for, they looked on with the idle stare of a bystander. Some few of the garrisons made a show of holding out; but, as Antony had left the whole of his army in Greece when he fled away after the battle of Actium, he had lost all chance of safety, and he put an end to his life by his sword. Cleopatra at first tried to carry her ships across the isthmus to the head of the Red Sea, and thence to fly to some unknown land from the power of the conqueror. She then tried to soften his heart by messages; but when she found that Octavianus only wanted her as an ornament to his triumphal show, she ended her life by poison, in the twenty-second B.C. 30. year of her reign, as the only means of escaping disgrace. Some later writers have said that she poisoned herself by the bite of an asp, as being the most easy way of dying; but for this there seems to be no authority. It is however curious to find that her physician Dioscorides, in his work on poisonous bites, says that the feelings at the time of death from the bite of an asp are rather pleasing than otherwise.

On the death of Antony, the struggle for the mastery of the Roman world was over. Octavianus, who had risen as the adopted heir of Julius Cæsar, felt however that the young Cæsarion stood

Lucanus,
lib. x. 360.
in his way. The flatterers of the conqueror would of course say
that Cæsarion was not the son of Julius, but of Ptolemy, the elder
of the two boys who had been called the husbands of Cleopatra.
The feelings of humanity might have added that he was the only
son of the uncle to whom Octavianus owed every thing; that he
was helpless and friendless, being cast off as illegitimate both by
Alexandria and by Rome; and that he never could trouble the un-
Plutarch.
Antony.
disputed master of the world.   But Octavianus, with the heartless
cruelty that murdered Cicero, and the cold caution which marked
his character through life, had Cæsarion at once put to death. As
he was then master of Rome, and able to drain Egypt of its treasures as easily, in the name of the senate, as Julius Cæsar and Antony had done in the name of the sovereign, he then declared the
Egyptian monarchy at an end, and the country in name and form,
what it had for some time been in reality, a province of Rome.

While we have in this history been looking at the Romans from
afar, and only seen their dealings with foreign kings, we have been
able to note some of the changes in their manners nearly as well
as if we had stood in the Forum. When Epiphanes, Philometor,
and Euergetes II. owed their crowns to Roman help, Rome gained
nothing but thanks, and that weight in their councils which is fairly
due to usefulness: the senate asked for no tribute, and the citizens
took no bribes. But with the growth of power came the love of
conquest and of its spoils. Macedonia was conquered in what might
be called self-defence; and, in the reign of Cleopatra Cocce, Cyrene
was won by fraud; Cyprus was then seized without a plea, and the
senators were even more eager for bribes than the senate for provinces. The nobles who governed these wide provinces grew too
powerful for the senate, and found that they could heap up ill-
gotten wealth faster by patronizing kings than by conquering them;

and the Egyptian monarchy was left to stand in the reigns of Auletes and Cleopatra, because the Romans were still more greedy
than when they seized Cyrene and Cyprus. Lastly, when Octavianus made himself autocrat of Rome, and thus gained for himself
whatever he seized in the name of the senate, he at once put an
end to the Egyptian monarchy.

Thus fell the family of the Ptolemies, a family that had perhaps
done more for arts and letters than any that can be pointed out in
history. Like other kings who have bought the praises of poets,
orators, and historians, they may have smothered the fire which
they seemed to foster, and have misled the talents which they wished
to guide; but in rewarding the industry of the mathematicians and
anatomists, of the critics, commentators, and compilers, they seem
to have been highly successful.

It is true that Alexandria never sent forth works with the high
tone of philosophy, the lofty moral aim, and the pure taste which
mark the writings of Greece in its best ages, and which ennoble the
mind and mend the heart; but it was the school to which the world
long looked for knowledge in all those sciences which help the body
and improve the arts of life, and which are sometimes called useful
knowledge. It was almost the birth-place of anatomy, geometry,
conic sections, geography, astronomy, and hydrostatics.

If we retrace the steps by which this Græco-Egyptian monarchy
rose and fell, we shall see that virtue and vice, wisdom and folly,
care and thoughtlessness were for the most part followed by the
rewards which to us seem natural.

We see in Ptolemy Soter plain manners, careful plans, untiring
activity, and a wise choice of friends. By him talents were highly

paid wherever they were found; no service left unrewarded; the people trusted and taught the use of arms, their love gained by wise laws and even-handed justice; docks, harbours, and fortresses built, schools opened; and by these means a great monarchy founded.

Ptolemy was eager to fill the ranks of his armies with soldiers, and his new city with traders. Instead of trying to govern against the will of the people, to thwart or overlook their wishes and feelings, his utmost aim was to guide them, and to make Alexandria a more agreeable place of settlement than the cities of Asia Minor and Syria, for the thousands who were then pouring out of Greece on the check given to its trading industry by the overthrow of its freedom. Though every thinking man must have seen that the new government when it gained shape and strength would be a military despotism, yet the people must have felt, while it was weak and resting on their good will rather than on their habits, that they were enjoying many of the blessings of freedom. Had they then claimed a share in the government they would most likely have gained it, and thereby they would have handed down those blessings to their children.

Before the death of Ptolemy Soter the habits of the people had so closely entwined themselves round the throne that Philadelphus was able to take the kingdom and the whole of its wide provinces at the hands of his father as a family estate. He did nothing to mar his father's wise plans which then ripened into fruit-bearing. Trade crowded the harbours and markets, learning filled the schools, conquests rewarded the discipline of the fleets and armies; power, wealth, and splendour followed in due order. The blaze thus cast around the throne would by many kings have been made to stand in the place of justice and mildness, but under Philadelphus it

only threw a light upon his good government. He was acknowledged both at home and abroad to be the first king of his age;
Greece and its philosophers looked up to him as a friend and patron;
and though as a man he must take rank far below his father, by
whose wisdom the eminence on which he stood was raised, yet in
all the gold and glitter of a king Philadelphus was the greatest of
his family.

The Egyptians had been treated with kindness by both of these
Greek kings. As far as they had been able or willing to copy the arts
of Greece they had been raised to a level with the Macedonians.
The Egyptian worship and temples had been upheld, as if in obe-
dience to the oft-repeated answer of the Delphic oracle, that the *Xenophon, Mem. iv. 3.*
gods should everywhere be worshipped according to the laws of
the country. But Euergetes was much more of an Egyptian, and
while he was restoring the ancient splendour to the temples, the
priests must have regained something of their former rank. But
they had no hold on the minds of the soldiers. Had the mercenaries upon whom the power of the king rested been worshippers
in the Egyptian temples, the priests might, as in the earlier times,
like a body of nobles, have checked his power when too great, and
at other times upheld it. Hence upon the whole, little seems to
have been gained by the court becoming more Egyptian, while the
army must have lost something of its Greek discipline and plainness of manners.

But in the next reign the fruits of this change were seen to be
most unfortunate. Philopator was an eastern despot, surrounded
by eunuchs and drowned in pleasures. The country was governed
by his women and vicious favourites. The army, which at the
beginning of his reign amounted to seventy-three thousand men
beside the garrisons, was at first weakened by rebellion, and before

the end of his reign it had fallen to pieces like a rope of sand. Nothing however happened to prove his weakness to surrounding nations; Egypt was still the greatest of kingdoms, though Rome on the conquest of Carthage, and Syria under Antiochus the Great, were fast gaining ground upon it; but he left to his infant son a throne shaken to the very foundations.

The ministers of Epiphanes, the infant autocrat, found the government without a head and without an army, the treasury without money, and the people without virtue or courage; and they at once threw the kingdom into the hands of the Romans, to save it from being shared between the kings of Syria and Macedonia. Thus passed the first five reigns, the first one hundred and fifty years, the first half of the three centuries that the kingdom of the Ptolemies lasted. It was then rotten at the core with vice and luxury. Its population was lessening, its trade falling off, its treasury empty, its revenue too small for the wasteful expenses of the government; but nevertheless, in the eyes of surrounding nations, its trade and wealth seemed boundless. Taste, genius, and poetry had passed away; but mathematics, surgery, and grammar still graced the Museum.

During the latter half of this history the kingdom was under the shield, but also under the sceptre of Rome. Its kings sent to Rome for help, sometimes against their enemies, and sometimes against their subjects; sometimes they humbly asked the senate for advice, and at other times were able respectfully to disobey the Roman orders. One by one the senate seized the provinces, Cœlo-Syria, the coast of Asia Minor, Cyrene, and the island of Cyprus; and lastly, though the Ptolemies still reigned, they were counted among the clients of the Roman patrician, to whom they looked up for patronage. From this low state Egypt could scarcely be said to fall when it became a part of the great empire of Augustus.

During these reigns the style of building, the religion, the writing, and the language of the Copts in the Thebaid were nearly the same as when their own kings were reigning in Thebes, with even fewer changes than usually creep in through time. They had all become less simple; and though it would be difficult and would want a volume by itself to trace these changes, and to show when they came into use, yet a few of them may be pointed out.

The change of fashion must needs be slow in buildings which are only raised by the untiring labour of years, and which when built stand for ages; but in the later temples we find less strength as fortresses, few obelisks or sphinxes, and no colossal statues or pyramids.

Into the religion there was brought a second Osiris, with a bull's head, as judge of the dead, named Serapis; a second Horus, with a hawk's head, which made it necessary to call the other one Aroëris, or the elder Horus; a second Anubis, with a dog's head, most likely the same god as Macedo, from whom the Macedonian kings were said to have sprung; while the trinities, or groups of three, into which these Egyptian polytheists, like the Hindoos, arranged their gods, became less common.

Many new characters crept into the hieroglyphics, as the came-lopard, the mummy lying on a couch, the ship with sails, and the chariot with horses; there were more words spelt with letters, the groups were more crowded, and the titles of the kings within the ovals became much longer.

With the papyrus, which was becoming common about the time of the Persian invasion, we find the running hand, the enchorial or common writing, as it was called, coming into use, in which there were few symbols, and most of the words were spelt with letters. Each letter was of the easy sloping form, which came from its being made with a reed or pen, instead of the stiff form of the hieroglyphics, which were mostly cut in stone. But there is a want of neatness which has thrown a difficulty over them, and made these writings less easy to read than the hieroglyphics.

Least of all can we trace the changes in the language, which is only really known to us through the Bible, which was translated into Coptic, with Greek letters, about two centuries after the fall of the Ptolemies. The language of the old hieroglyphics seems to have been nearly the same as this, but they must be much better understood than they are before we can point out the changes in the language in which they were written.

When the country fell into the hands of Augustus, the Copts were in a much lower state than when conquered by Alexander. They had been slaves for three hundred years, sometimes trusted and well-treated, but more often trampled on and ground down with taxes and cruelty. They had never held up their heads as freemen or felt themselves lords of their own soil: they had fallen off in numbers, in wealth, and in knowledge: nothing was left to them but their religion, their temples, their hieroglyphics, and the painful remembrance of their faded glories.

THE END.

INDEX OF NAMES.

SVB ALA.

LONDON:

PRINTED BY ARTHUR TAYLOR, COLEMAN STREET.

1838.